TO: TONI
FROM: JEFF

MW00799213

The Hostility Of Change
Breaking Through Deep-Seated Barriers

Joe Robert Thornton

The Hostility Of Change
Breaking Through Deep-Seated Barriers
All Rights Reserved.
Copyright © 2021 Joe Robert Thornton
v9.0

The opinions expressed in this manuscript are solely the opinions of the author and do not represent the
opinions or thoughts of the publisher. The author has represented and warranted full ownership and/or legal
right to publish all the materials in this book.

This book may not be reproduced, transmitted, or stored in whole or in part by any means, including graphic,
electronic, or mechanical without the express written consent of the publisher except in the case of brief
quotations embodied in critical articles and reviews.

Vizzionnary Publishing

Paperback ISBN: 978-0-578-24193-7
Hardback ISBN: 978-0-578-24194-4

Cover Photo © 2021 www.gettyimages.com. All rights reserved - used with permission.

PRINTED IN THE UNITED STATES OF AMERICA

The Chapters

Some details and names have been changed to protect the privacy of individuals. Some characters, businesses, places, events, and incidents are used in a fictitious manner. Events and conversations have been recreated from memory.

Although the author and publisher have made every effort to ensure that the information in this book was correct at the time of press, the author and publisher do not assume any liability to any party for any loss, damage, or impact caused by errors or omissions.

Real, sustainable change is difficult...
but not impossible.

This book is dedicated to my wife, Inez Thornton. She has endured more change than any human being that I know. Physical change, mental change, and emotional change... and sometimes all at once. She has encouraged me and empowered me to be able to manage any change that comes my way.

"The moment that a moment is gone, change has occurred."

~ Joe Robert Thornton

Foreword

Change is a topic that Joe Thornton has been passionate about for a long time. I know because I had the opportunity to participate in his early leadership journey almost twenty years ago as an independent consultant. I got to see up close and personal how Joe navigated change to help transform the operation of a 5,500 store, multi-billion dollar organization. Without explicit line authority, Joe was able to diplomatically lead a large group of field coaches to implement significant operational changes across the entire country successfully.

Through that experience and so many other leadership opportunities in the ensuing years, Joe has learned much about change. He has invested a great deal of time and energy into his professional career and, over the years, has experienced a multitude of approaches to change management... a competency that he views as, arguably, the most challenging aspect of leadership. Joe believes that there is a hostility in the change process, an often deep-seated resistance that needs to be better understood. He also believes that unlocking that opposition, that hostility, can help accelerate the trajectory of change.

But Joe has learned that change is not just about process. He sees change as an emotional journey that people experience, and the role of leadership is to inspire people to want to make that change. He also believes that change, contrary to many organizational applications, is not a team sport... every individual must go through the change process on their own.

In his broad operational roles, Joe has seen the change management approach demonstrated with a variety of outcomes. Some of the change management attempts have been successful at embedding real, sustainable change in an organization, but equally, Joe has observed attempts at change that completely missed the mark. Not only was the organization unable to implement the expected change, but as a result of the failed endeavor, the institution's culture and trust were seriously fractured.

Joe also believes that before the professional journey of change can begin, the personal journey of change must occur. He also recognizes that the more that we can overcome personal change challenges... things as simple as eating healthier or exercising consistently... the better we can equip ourselves as leaders to help others through change.

In this book, Joe explores what is required in each of us to achieve personal change and, eventually, leadership growth. He has taken the time to weave together the experiences and lessons that he has learned and tells real-life stories about change and the impact that they have had on people and the businesses that they led. Joe takes on the deep-seated barriers to change and offers recommendations to help individuals and organizations break through the frequent resentment associated with change.

And finally, Joe introduces principles that challenge the traditional ways of thinking about change management.

Ultimately, I know that Joe would like to see everyone have success in making real, sustainable change in their lives. Taking the time to share his personal experiences in this manner is his way of giving back to others- to those who have invested in his leadership journey and those who are struggling with change in their everyday lives.

Mitch Telson
Former Chief Operating Officer- Circle K
Former President- Petco

Preface

I recognize that hostility is a strong word. Just hearing the word can stir emotions.

Hostility, by definition, is emotionally charged aggression. Hostility is the state of ill will and bad feelings. Hostility is unfriendly, animosity, bad blood, antagonism, belligerence, rancor.

I titled this book The Hostility Of Change. In part because change can be all these things too.

I also chose this title because change is not always what it appears to be. It does not always go along with the nicely-packaged processes that we have developed.

Let me explain: Change is often presented as a symbiotic process that happens, many times amongst teams, and with the expectation that everyone will be on board with the change. The reality is that change is rarely symbiotic; each person must go through change, and to get to effective change implementation, I believe that you must assume that the change will *not* be willingly accepted- that there will be hostility.

Here is the reason why:

Change brings out emotion. Sometimes outwardly demonstrated, sometimes even in a hostile way.

Change can also invoke a passively hostile resistance, often difficult to detect, but just as detrimental to the change process you are attempting to implement. Best-in-class leaders recognize this and address it just as aggressively as they address the overt resistance to change.

Regardless of how it is demonstrated, change is part and parcel to the human experience. We are constantly changing and constantly experiencing change. As a result, change is everywhere, and we are always attempting to solve it.

This constant process makes change tricky. In part, because I do not believe that change is a static continuum, moving from one phase to another until it is accepted. I will discuss this more later in the book.

On the professional side of change, organizations spend millions of dollars every year putting their teams through change management training, even hiring outside consultants to lead the process. The number of activities, meetings, seminars, events, training materials, and manuals dedicated to change management can be overwhelming.

In the end, many organizations and leaders come to the same fork in the road related to change management- they launch new programs and processes only to find weeks or months later that real, sustainable change did not occur. The new techniques that were introduced to their teams did not get embedded, and old behaviors returned. It leaves many organizations dissecting their approach and trying to understand what they could have done differently.

In part, I believe that this is because real, sustainable change happens deep down inside of each person. Let me be clear, activities created to inspire people to want to change are not wrong, they are just not effective. Why?

I am carefully choosing my words here:

Leaders can inspire people to want to change, but leaders cannot make people change.

Ultimately, there must be a catalyst for change... internally. Not some writing on the wall that was cleverly crafted by the corporate office think-tank or worse, by outside consultants hired by the organization that know even less about the actual people who need to be inspired to believe in the change.

Not real, sustainable change anyway. There is a distinction here that I will get to later in the book.

On the personal side of change, many of us have embarked on a life journey of start and stop changes- whether it is around relationships, exercise, diets, etc. We are continually pushing to change and be better- many times finding ourselves back where we started. On some level, changing our behavior should be easier than attempting to change a team of people you are leading. So, it would seem.

However, personal change can be even more difficult simply because there is no one else to blame if the change is not implemented.

Professionally, I have gone through many iterations of change management processes in my career, and virtually none of them achieved the desired success in any organization that I worked. While it is not my intention, I recognize that this sounds a bit negative and broad-sweeping. However, I am only amplifying how difficult real, sustainable change is to achieve. That said, when the change was successful, the common denominator was exceptional leadership... always exceptional leadership. But back to when it did not work...

In my experiences, either the change did not reach enough people to influence an overall change, the change took too long to implement, or the change did not stay in place long enough for the organization to realize the benefits of the change.

In reflection, there were many culprits. A fair amount of it was due to a flawed approach and perhaps unrealistic expectations. Do not get me wrong; you should be optimistic about change, but not naïve. The larger the group, the more likely someone is actively working to sabotage the change for their own reasons. Sabotage- such a provocative word- I am going to come back to that later.

Another culprit is when all the change work was driven from the outside looking in or from the top down. The buy-in will likely be low when this happens, reducing the probability of success.

In the organizations that I had worked for, when things did not work, we were often left with this unyielding question to answer- "Why didn't the change stick?"

All that said, I remain optimistic about implementing real, sustainable change. Why?

Leadership, of course.

Back to the point- leaders can inspire people to want to change, but leaders cannot make people change.

With the right injection of inspiration though, anything is possible. Inspiration, however, should not be conflated with crises, ultimatums, or other maxims that drive compliance instead of real commitment to change. For example:

You may have heard of the term 'The Burning Platform'- a business lexicon, coined by Daryl Conner in his 1993 book, "Managing At The Speed Of Change," that emphasizes immediate and radical change due to dire circumstances.

I will share the quick story that Conner tells in the book.

The origin of the term 'The Burning Platform' comes from a story about a man on the North Sea Piper Alpha oil rig that caught on fire in 1988.

At nine-thirty on a July evening in 1988, a disastrous explosion occurred on an oil-drilling platform in the North Sea off the coast of Scotland. One hundred and sixty-six people lost their lives in the worst catastrophe in the twenty-five-year history of North Sea oil exploration. One of the sixty-three crew members who survived was a superintendent named Andy Mochan.

From his hospital bed, Andy told of being awakened by the explosion and subsequent alarms. He said that he ran from his quarters to the platform edge and jumped fifteen stories from the platform to the water. Because of the frigid water temperature, Andy knew that he could live a maximum of only twenty minutes if he were not rescued. Also, oil had surfaced and caught fire. Despite the dangerous fire below, Andy jumped one hundred and fifty feet in the middle of the night into an ocean of burning oil and debris.

When asked why he took that potentially fatal leap, Andy did not hesitate. He said, "It was either jump or fry."

Andy chose possible death over certain death.

He did not jump because he felt confident that he would survive. In his calculation, he jumped because he had no choice— the price of staying on the platform, maintaining the status quo, was too high.

Fortunately, Andy did survive the jump from the platform and was rescued by boat shortly thereafter.

The story's point is that it took a platform that was literally on fire to cause a significant change in behavior. This story emphasizes that radical change in people usually only comes when a dire situation presents itself, and the consequences of doing nothing become too great.

When making significant decisions or solving major problems, sometimes a radical approach is necessary to break us out of our normal tendencies.

This story is a powerful metaphor. It is hard to hear this story without mentally placing yourself on the edge of a burning oil rig, thinking about what you would do if you were in that situation.

In today's evolving business environment, more and more organizations are finding themselves on a burning platform. Leaders face a status quo that they can no longer afford- some being forced to change by stakeholders- internal and external, and some being forced to change for dollars and cents reasons. Although dramatic change may be disruptive and sometimes expensive, organizations feeling the pressure recognize and believe that change is no longer optional and, therefore, must be embraced... and this was all before the coronavirus outbreak.

It would be easy for me to write about the pandemic in this book and tuck it under a crisis headline. On the other hand, it would be somewhat irresponsible to write a book about change and leave the coronavirus pandemic out altogether.

After all, the virus created a lot of change. Change that no one saw coming, change that no one liked, and change that created a new way of living. Or did it? I am not sure what stage of the pandemic that we will be in at the printing of this book. The reality is that it does not matter because the coronavirus pandemic forced change instead of inspiring change. The virus represented a problem that was difficult to solve for sure, but it also embodied everything that is wrong about change. The key takeaway for me that puts change and crisis at odds is:

Real, sustainable change is a level above crisis.

What that means is that, when the threat of the crisis is gone, people will likely revert to old behaviors... which is why we are always at risk for a pandemic. I know, not what you want to hear.

Take a deep breath...

Okay, back to the burning platform. The approach that you decide to implement to make change happen is the real challenge, and being able to thread the needle doing so is what separates real, sustainable change from an organization ending up needing to have a do-over... or worse, becoming irrelevant and ultimately out of business.

A real burning platform does not give the option of the status quo. A burning platform is not a simulation- it is real, it is happening, and it requires action.

A burning platform is a situation where all options are dire, but you must still choose. This is a critical call-out because, without dire consequences, you are not often compelled to take action.

The point that I ultimately want to get to here with this story is this:

The challenge of real, sustainable change is creating urgency, without manufacturing it, without waiting for a catastrophic event, without forcing it, and getting people to change because they want to change. That is asking a lot, but that is necessary for real, sustainable change to occur.

You can come across as disingenuous if there is always a dire situation in your business that you are presenting to your team and one that tricks your team into doing it only because they feel that they have no choice.

Anyway, many of you know what happens when you make someone do something they do not want to do. If you are a parent with teenagers that have put you at your wit's end or if you can remember the pain that you may have put your parents through as a teenager, then you know that forced change does not work so well.

In the end, you should not want to force people to change. It will only get you to compliance with little chance of getting to commitment. Instead, through inspiration and involvement, you want people to look forward to making the change.

Real, sustainable change is a high bar- a remarkably high bar.

Let me talk for a moment about the subtitle- "Breaking Through Deep-Seated Barriers."

First, this term is often referred to as "deep-seeded." Deep-seeded almost metaphorically makes more sense, but the correct term is actually "deep-seated." The phrase also had an earlier literal meaning of "situated far below the surface," as in "a deep-seeded inflammation." The figurative use of the word was born from that meaning, and the incorrect spelling of "deep-seeded" developed.

The most fundamental meaning of deep-seated is something that is firmly established, as in a seat. That makes a better link to the correct term of "deep-seated."

Deep-seated is relevant to the topic of change because the position that people have before they go through change is often driven by deeply-entrenched views that have been formed over a long period. So deeply entrenched to the point that even contrary, factual information may not move people off their position when change is presented.

Acknowledging these deep-seated views is vital as you implement any change process. These factors, in aggregate, often result in change-resistant responses that sound something like this:

> "This is the way it's always been done."
> "Things are fine the way that they are."
> "If it is not broke, don't fix it."
> "We tried that before, and it didn't work."

Did I miss any? I am sure there are more. They all get you to the same place- an incredibly low likelihood of change occurring.

These eight-word statements often cause less confident and less competent leaders to fold up like a tent under the pressure of implementing change and ultimately overcoming resistance. If you are not prepared to make a case for why things are not 'fine' in the current state and how they can be better in the future state, change will be elusive.

In this book, I examine what it takes for willing change to occur that will create sustainable behaviors that allow your organization to break through the hostility that comes with change and continue to move forward. By the way, this also applies to your personal life and to that twenty pounds that you told yourself that you would lose last year. I am just saying...

Your response to change can change change.

Oh, I love good alliteration. I know, technically, it is repetition, but alliteration sounds so much cooler for this example.

How you respond to and lead through change has everything to do with what the outcome will be. Do not underestimate the altered state of change that authentic leadership can impact.

In the end, I am writing a book about change, not <u>the</u> book about change. No one can truly write <u>the</u> book because change will continue to happen while the book is being written.

I hope that this book helps you get to the grounds truth about change and opens your mind to the possibilities of real, sustainable change.

I also hope that the examples in the book help unlock new thinking for you in your personal life and as a leader of others.

CHAPTER 1:

Change Is An Emotion

I will open with this. It is one of my foundational beliefs. One that sets the stage for why change is so difficult:

Change is not a process. Change is an emotion.

This may sound logical, yet we almost always arrive at the same place with change implementation strategies- a group sitting around the table rolling out a new program heavily focused on processes, tools, manuals, and timelines.

Because so much energy is committed to processes, the group leading the change often cannot see the value in investing time anticipating emotional responses. As important, that usually means little time spent equipping leaders with how to respond, support, and keep the change train moving. Even time developing frequently asked questions, talking to front-line employees, and anticipating problems are often ignored.

There is always a reason why many of these steps are left out...

and almost every one of them you will be addressing after the fact if you do not address them upfront.

I will say this: I do not view this behavior as intentionally malicious. At times, I see leaders who can no longer put themselves in the place of the people that they are leading to anticipate the barriers to change. Not being able to remember what it feels like to go through experiences that others are now faced with is a dangerous tenet of leadership in many aspects, but it can be fatal when it comes to change.

So back to this:
Change is not a process. Change is an emotion.

Almost everything that I see connected to business has a process. Many of these processes are essential to the continuity of execution. And yes, processes are also necessary to change management. When attempting to launch change across a large group of people, or even when you are working on building new routines in your personal life, process will help you facilitate the steps needed to make it happen.

What I have learned, though, is that no matter how artfully done, a process is still a process.

It is simply impossible to put emotions on a checklist or into a binder.
Think of it this way- the binder, the checklist, the processes are essential, but you must inspire people to want to open them and use them.

Conversely, we are human beings, and emotions play a large part in almost all our decision-making, choices, and reactions. The actual attempt to engineer processes absent from emotional considerations is a risk that needs to be considered as you prepare to undergo a significant change. This is an incubator for hostility.

To this point, though, if you think about change as an emotion, you begin to plan differently, anticipate differently, even react differently.

This approach becomes even more critical when change is not embedded... and, by the way, it is likely that, with the ebb and flow of life, you will experience change that does not get embedded in your personal life and your professional life.

When change does not stick in your personal life or an organizational role, there can be multiple reasons, and it is likely that at least one of those reasons is connected to emotions. If you do not address the emotional part of the change, you risk getting compliance, not commitment.

Senior leaders of organizational change often blame implementation failures on employee and middle manager resistance to change. At times, this is true. At times though, it is because emotions were never factored into the implementation plan. Senior leaders and managers often overestimate how much change they can force on the organization. Some also do not understand how difficult it is to lead and implement change effectively... because of emotions.

This is another point where you must strike a balance. Here is what I mean:

The best-in-class leaders understand that being able to demonstrate emotions such as empathy and compassion are critical. In fact:

Empathy and compassion are allies of change.

This topic needs a chapter of its own, so I will break down empathy and compassion later in the book.

When people feel like you are emotionally invested with them, they are more likely to embrace the change that you are presenting to them. To be clear, I am not recommending that this is a guarantee that they will embrace the change, just an improvement of the probability of it occurring.

Best-in-class leaders also recognize that demonstrating that they understand how this change will feel can be a strong connection point. Even using terms like 'I remember when' can be powerful in connecting with those you lead through the change, but be careful. This is only effective when it connects authentically.

I will digress to share an example and emphasize why striking a balance is material to this point:

Try using 'I remember when' on your teenage child in a conversation, then let me know how that worked out for you- I believe I already know the answer.

You believe that you are sharing a valuable life lesson with your child that will serve them well. After all, you care enough to not want them to make the same mistakes you did at their age.

It all makes sense except... all your child heard was, "Back in the stone age, I walked ten miles uphill both ways to school... in the snow, with no shoes..."

I actually did walk seven miles home in the snow in the ninth grade from basketball practice. However, I did have shoes on. Anyway...

Your comments to your child, with such authentic intention, likely did not connect. The point is that 'I remember when' is not for every situation. If it is not authentic and useful, do not be surprised if you get a hostile response.

Of course, with a teenager, you could get a hostile response no matter how well you approach a conversation. Listen, I recognize that there is a bit of bias in that statement... and I am okay with that. I have had three children go through the teenage timeline already. While it does not make me an expert, it gives me the credibility to speak on the topic.

However, whenever 'I remember when' or similar comments connect, they can make all the difference. I have written before about pragmatism as part of the art of leadership. In a sense, the demonstration of realism and practicality can be strikingly relatable to your workforce, mostly because this is how many of your people live every day. Pragmatism can demonstrate your ability to be empathetic or compassionate.

People in your organization will believe that you understand their plight. This understanding is key as it will prevent your messages from getting lost in translation because of unrealistic expectations and beliefs. It also bolsters the odds for change to happen... and stick.

So, factoring in emotions is vital... but do it authentically.

Emotions are so critical to change management that some of the most effective change leaders do not even appeal to a process. Instead, they appeal to emotions. Sure, they have processes in place, but what you see, what they emphasize, and ultimately what makes them successful is the interest in demonstrating emotion to meet people where they are and even allowing emotional responses during the change process.

You see it in sports with a coach attempting to spark a behavior change. Coaches that yell at their players are not always yelling at their players- they are clamoring to get a response, a change in behavior.

For example, a basketball coach may "intentionally" get a technical foul to get their team's emotions to rise to their emotional level and play harder. The coach is making a calculated decision to potentially get ejected from the game with the belief that it could inspire their team to play harder... and there are occasions where it works.

Even when a coach is yelling at a player, they are often making a calculated decision in that situation as well. They understand what motivates each player, and for some, it creates the right spark.

You also see this play out in a classroom where a teacher demonstrates an uncharacteristic emotion to get a change in behavior from their students. This is not always a more aggressive emotion like anger; it could be sadness or vulnerability.

The teacher realizes that a different approach, involving emotion, may cause the students to pay more attention than they usually do. In this situation, the teacher is making a bet on the students reacting, perhaps questioning what is wrong with the teacher or questioning what happened to the teacher that is creating this different behavior. Once the teacher has the attention of the students, the likelihood of introducing change increases.

Lastly, you also see this in the boardroom of some of the most successful companies. Best-in-class leaders understand that emotions, strategically used, can move teams to achieve what was previously thought to be unattainable.

A team seeing an emotional reaction from their leader can inspire each member of the team to look introspectively at their performance and contribution and take ownership of delivering more.

Leaders often viewed as pragmatic are likely to get more of a reaction when demonstrating emotional leadership- whether that is anger on one end of the spectrum or compassion on the other end of the spectrum. Said differently, if you rarely show emotion, any demonstration of emotion is likely to be noticed and get more of a reaction. In general, moving away from your center of emotions will likely draw a response.

At times, if you are already an emotionally-charged leader, it could be more challenging to move to a more noticeable emotional approach. That said, I believe that people generally feel authentic leadership. Even with a minimal change in emotion, you could still generate a reaction that helps change the trajectory of behaviors or results you are looking to achieve.

Let me stop here and acknowledge that you may be thinking about leaders who are just as effective at change that do not use emotion... or maybe it appears that they do not use emotion. Two things to get to here:

First, we are sometimes conditioned to think about emotions only as anger, yelling, crying- more visceral and visible emotions. That is okay. Again, even when leaders are yelling and demonstrating anger, the delivery may look and feel harmful, but others may be inspired by it.

Okay, wait. I know that may seem counterintuitive. If I were reading this out loud to you, I would expect someone to stop me and ask me to explain. So, what do I mean by this?

I mentioned the example of a basketball coach yelling but let me go more in-depth on another example.

If you have ever attended a Southern Baptist church on Sunday morning, I am referring to the 11:00 am service that is not followed by another service, you recognize that you could be there all day. The pastor usually takes advantage of that. Cynical, I know.

Listen, this is not every Southern Baptist pastor. Still, I have attended enough services intermittently growing up and over the years, and there are enough examples of this to call it more than just a stereotype.

If you attend a Southern Baptist service for the first time from another type of church service, you may be caught off guard by the amount of emotion demonstrated by the pastor. It usually involves preaching, of course, but preaching means yelling, sweating, and almost admonishing the church congregation at times. This delivery and behavior may feel negative to a visitor, but this can be incredibly inspiring to the every-Sunday-member. The pastor's righteous message is just what many congregation members need to feel compelled to repent. It gives them the energy to face the upcoming week.

Okay, if you have never experienced that, that example will not resonate with you.

So, here is another one:

Think about your local spin class instructor, or your yoga class instructor, or your personal trainer. It is possible that you have seen them demonstrate emotion, specifically yelling, and yet that authority could be precisely what you need. It does not come off to you as negative; it is inspiring. You recognize that you cannot get there on your own, so you are okay with this type of aggression- you are literally paying for it.

That is one end of the spectrum. However, change leaders also exhibit compassion, empathy, authenticity, connectedness- a display of behavior that may not be technically defined as an emotion, but creates emotion in the people they are leading.

Ultimately, in both types of emotions, the leaders are setting the stage for change to occur.

The second part of this is using appropriate emotion in the proper place and time.

There is a saying that leaders should "act like a duck." It speaks to a quote attributed to Jacob M. Braude- "Always behave like a duck- keep calm and unruffled on the surface, but paddle like the devil underneath."

I have always thought about this quote in two ways:

One, the very image of a duck gliding effortlessly across a pond, creating barely a ripple in the water, is a thing of beauty- it can build a calm inside of us. The violent paddling underneath can be a metaphor for all the hard work that has gone into making the above the water, what most often we see, look effortless. I believe that is true of almost anyone in a line of entertainment, sports, and other crafts. We see the end result, but rarely the hard work that went into it.

The other way that I have interpreted this quote is more akin to leadership and this conversation:

I believe that a leader's number one responsibility is to inspire, which means demonstrating behaviors that tie people emotionally to the company, especially on the business's front line (the duck on the surface). Doing so is more likely to create an environment for people to want to change when change is introduced. A leader who leads with a calm, steady hand at the very least gets the benefit of potentially higher productivity because the team is focused on the work instead of what mood the leader is in at any given time. Now, let me counteract all that and define that as just table stakes. That is how good leaders should behave.

There is more to this, though. 'Acting like a duck' may also make the leader appear more approachable and open the door for problems to be considered a good thing. Above all else, though, it is about being relatable, creating authentic connections, and inspiring the team.

In the second part of the quote, behind the scenes, that same leader may need to demonstrate different leadership behaviors. Perhaps a more direct, coarse approach to effect change to get work done (the duck underneath). The violent paddling underneath is perhaps a euphemism for an emotionally charged conversation behind closed doors that needs to take place for change to happen.

Neither is better than the other, merely different for different situations.

A part of our reaction to change is based on our emotions. Our emotions are based on our biases. Our biases determine to what degree that we embrace the change being introduced.

Wow- bias. Now there is a small word with huge implications on the change process. We will get to that in a later chapter.

As I became a student of change, one of the most impactful books that I read early in my career was "Six Thinking Hats." It was written more than thirty-five years ago, but it still reads relevant today.

In summary, "Six Thinking Hats" is a system designed by Edward de Bono, which describes a tool for group discussion and individual thinking involving six colored hats. "Six Thinking Hats" provides an approach for groups to plan thinking processes in a detailed and cohesive way and, in doing so, to think together more effectively.

The premise of the method is that the human brain thinks in many distinct ways, which can be deliberately challenged. In each of these directions, the brain will identify and bring into conscious thought certain aspects of issues being considered (e.g., intuition, pessimism, neutral facts).

Colored hats are used as metaphors for each direction of thinking. Switching to a different approach is symbolized by putting on a colored hat, either literally or metaphorically. These metaphors allow for more complete and elaborate segregation of the thinking directions.

The six colored hats are:

> The White Hat- information, facts
> The Yellow Hat- brightness and optimism
> The Black Hat- judgment, devil's advocate
> The Red Hat- feelings, emotions, intuition
> The Green Hat- creativity
> The Blue Hat- manages the thinking process

I took a couple of my teams through the book years ago and the subsequent exercises practicing the use of the hats. The relatable point here is that, in using each of the hats, I found myself most fascinated by the Red Hat. The Red Hat is about emotions, and hostility is an emotion.

The hat that most members of both teams struggled with using was the Red Hat. Because of that, I found myself stopping the process when we arrived there. I wanted to understand what they were going through when practicing with the Red Hat.

There were many reasons why this hat often seemed to be the most uncomfortable to utilize:

One, most of the team grew up with the instilled belief that emotions and business do not go together, that it is not professional. Even in the safe environment of a simple role-play, it still felt uncomfortable for most of them. Overall, skepticism about allowing emotions in the business setting blanketed the process.

Second, for those who are not naturally emotional, it was even more difficult. Attempting to demonstrate anger when you are not actually angry, and you are not accustomed to expressing anger, was a stretch for many on the team. For those in that position on the team, it felt disingenuous.

Lastly, there was an uneasy feeling of not needing to justify your position when using the Red Hat- you do not have to be positive; you do not need facts, you just share how you feel. The intuition aspect of the Red Hat was a challenge for many- a feeling of making decisions by "the seat of your pants" and again, not needing to justify it. This produced cynicism- can you really do this and get away with it in the 'real world?'

For me, the process amplified the point that we do not have a consistent way of dealing with emotions in the workplace, and if we even should- then and now.

Allowing emotions in business is sometimes viewed as the leader being "out of control." Quite the contrary- allowing emotions in business can be a demonstration of confident leadership.

Emotions are essential, yet there is a tendency to shy away from them and even suppress them in a business setting. I am not saying that it is wrong to believe that, but I think doing this misses the opportunity to create an optimal environment for people to be their authentic selves.

More importantly, for this conversation, attempting to lead a change process without demonstrating emotion may unknowingly push the team even further away from the change process. You may come across as heavy process-oriented and, again, unknowingly cause the team to suppress their emotions throughout the change.

It is always important to be authentic above all else as a leader- you should never attempt to manufacture emotions. This could also serve to turn the team away from the change and even away from your leadership.

If you are experiencing emotions related to the change- either how you felt when you first heard about the change, where you had to overcome your struggle with the change, or just acknowledging that the change may be challenging, it is important to share it. The last thing you want in a change process is to be void of emotion and come across as robotic.

Let me go back up to the top level of this discussion about emotions.

Although everyone experiences emotions, scientists do not even agree on what emotions are or how they should be measured. Emotions are complex and have both physical and mental components.

The good news is that people, in general, have very similar responses to the same emotion. For example, regardless of age, race, or gender, when people are under stress, their bodies release adrenaline. Adrenaline creates reactions like a racing heartbeat or sweating.

Of course, it is relatively easy to spot physical emotions like pain. We often touch, hold, or reference pain areas differently, including even how we walk at times. With physical pain, we often emit expressive behaviors that are demonstrated when emotion is being experienced.

Outward signs of emotions can also provide clues to others about what we are experiencing, such as muscle tensing when angry and facial expressions to denote emotion, like crying. Also, our tone of voice can demonstrate a wide range of emotions.

The component of emotions that scientists call subjective feelings refers to how each person experiences feelings, which is the most difficult to describe or measure.

Subjective feelings are more challenging, as they cannot be observed. Instead, the person experiencing the emotion must describe it to others, and each person's description and interpretation of a feeling may be different.

For example, two people falling in love will not experience or describe their feeling in the same way. The degree to which someone is experiencing an emotion like love cannot be fully articulated. To go further, those who have not experienced the feeling being described literally cannot relate to what they are hearing. For those that have experienced that emotion, their level of intensity will determine how well they do connect to what is being described.

In a business setting, emotional reactions to change are a normal response to the real and perceived disruption that accompanies organizational change. Successful change leaders know that understanding and addressing the mixed emotions that employees may experience can help employees feel motivated, inspired, and willing to support the change.

And yet, some organizations still believe that expressing emotions should be actively discouraged. This is another point where emotions tie back to the change process. It can be tempting to automatically interpret the mixed feelings that people express as resistance to change, and to view resistance as something negative, to be 'dealt with.' Employees may be expected to hide their emotions. Employees who feel the need to hide their feelings for fear of being labeled a 'resistor' may end up pretending to comply with intended changes. There is a term to describe this called "covering." I will discuss covering on this change journey.

Working in organizations often means that we must leave our emotions at the door as we enter our place of work... or should we? Many of us have even been explicitly told to check our emotions at the door when arriving at work.

Let us think about that for a moment. We are emotional beings, and when we arrive at work, expecting us to be someone or something different can be extremely dangerous... and unrealistic. In fact, I believe the best-in-class leaders do just the opposite. They encourage people to bring their entire, authentic selves to work. These leaders understand that bringing out the whole person can create an emotional connection throughout their team and, in turn, create greater connections with their customers.

Even if this cannot be scientifically proven, it certainly presents a case for building trusting relationships at work. Again, on this change journey, you want people to want to make the change.

Anyway, making people do anything against their will feels like a demand. If you are in a leadership position at work or even in a personal situation where you have power over another person, that demand may sound like an ultimatum.

CHAPTER 2:

The Ultimatum

Presenting someone with an ultimatum is likely to create hostility.

An ultimatum is defined as a threat in which a person is warned that if they do not do a particular thing, something unpleasant will happen to them. It is usually the last and most extreme in a series of actions taken to bring about a specific result.

You may be thinking that an ultimatum sounds very much like a burning platform. One key distinction is that an ultimatum does not have to be accompanied by an immediate, dire situation- it is merely a demand to do something, with or without the urgency of a timeline.

For some, change itself, of any kind, is an ultimatum. An ultimatum can create change... which means that an ultimatum can generate emotion... but perhaps not the emotion you desire.

When you thrust change upon someone, by surprise, without consent, without alignment, and without agreement, it is basically an ultimatum… and you should, at the very least, anticipate a hostile response.

When the only way that an organization can create the commitment necessary to implement change successfully is to present an ultimatum- we do this or else we face a consequence, do not be surprised by the visceral reaction that you get to the change.

So, what do I mean by that? Well, I can best describe the impact of an ultimatum by telling you a story:

Such was the case with one of the most revered American brands of the last half-century- Blockbuster Video.

It is rare that an ultimatum of scale in business is a success, and no, I am not going to tell you that the Blockbuster ultimatum was a success. You already know how this story ended but let me tell you about how they got here.

Blockbuster proposed the ultimatum of all ultimatums… and then paid a heavy price for it.

I know, tantalizing headline. Let me set some context first.

I worked for Blockbuster when it was cool to work for Blockbuster. I was there for the 'good years' between 1992 and 2006. Blockbuster had begun to grow significantly by 1992 and had not yet entirely crashed by 2006. However, a lot happened during those fourteen years that set the stage for the meteoric rise and, ultimately, the sensational fall of the brand, resulting in just four more years of operation after I left.

Most people on the outside looking in believe that Netflix and Redbox are what took Blockbuster down. Well, not exactly. In fact, it was more of the ultimatum... and of course, this thing called hubris- just a fancy word for excessive pride or arrogance.

Netflix did play a role, though... but only because of hubris.

Let me start by saying that Netflix today looks nothing like Netflix of 2000- nothing. I do not want to make this chapter about Netflix, but it does serve as a sharp dichotomy to what happened to Blockbuster.

It is hard to imagine now, but Netflix was fighting for relevance at the start of the 2000s. It burned through more than fifty million dollars in 2000, struggled to hit 300,000 subscribers, and had to forgo their plans to go public. Needing help, Netflix turned to an improbable source- Blockbuster.

In 2000, Reed Hastings, the co-founder of Netflix, flew to Dallas to propose a partnership with Blockbuster. The idea was that Netflix would operate the Blockbuster brand online, and Blockbuster would take a 50% stake in Netflix and promote Netflix in its stores. Together, they would expand the up-and-coming DVD subscription service- one that Blockbuster was struggling to launch. It seems like a great idea now. However, you must remember where we were twenty years ago. Blockbuster had all the leverage in the industry, and it was silly even to consider sharing the spotlight with anyone else, let alone a start-up company. So, no, in 2000, it seemed like a stupid idea.

Blockbuster management ultimately said, and I am paraphrasing, "Why would we do that? We know more about the business than you do. If it is such a good business, we'll do it ourselves." Of course, Blockbuster did try to do it themselves- I was there front and center for that- and we failed spectacularly. It certainly was not for lack of effort, but honestly, we did not know what the hell we were doing. We might as well have been attempting to put a man on the moon. Actually, that would have been easier. We were so outside of our element, and we did not know how to ask for help. Hubris.

In the end, you know how the story turned out. Today, Netflix rules the entertainment landscape with 130 million subscribers in nearly 200 countries, a growing slate of award-winning programming, and a market cap of more than $150 billion... and that was before the boom in streaming services as a result of the coronavirus. The crisis pushed the Netflix market cap to over $200 billion due to an additional $50 billion gain... in just the first full quarter of the coronavirus pandemic!

On the other hand, Blockbuster has one store on the entire planet that is still in operation. I visited there last year. I will get to that experience later in the book.

Netflix outmaneuvered Blockbuster by quickly reacting to emerging shifts in technology. When Netflix launched in 1997, it bet everything on DVDs even though VHS was the industry standard. Then it invested in streaming when its focus groups showed consumers knew so little about the concept that they often misrepresented the term "streaming" by saying "streamlining." People fumed at Netflix in 2011 for its plans to split streaming and DVDs into two services. Hundreds of thousands of customers canceled their subscriptions in the months that followed.

While these ideas may have been premature or poorly rolled out, they demonstrated the courage to go there. Netflix bolted ahead of the major video rental chains, capitalized on faster internet delivery for streaming videos, and spent billions outbidding traditional studios for original movies and television shows, starting with "House of Cards."

If foresight and focus were vital to Netflix's survival, so was the delayed response of its more established rival. Blockbuster did not challenge Netflix with an online DVD rental service of its own until 2004. It took another two years before Blockbuster let customers return online rentals in stores, making the service more convenient and a more significant threat to Netflix. When it did get going, Blockbuster quickly topped two million subscribers by the end of 2006, or nearly half of Netflix's subscriber base at the time. But Netflix execs remained convinced the venture was too costly for Blockbuster to sustain. Sure enough, Blockbuster raised prices after barely a year and cut its marketing budget for the service.

In the end, for the role that Netflix played in potentially accelerating the demise, Blockbuster certainly could have done something different about that at that time.

It seems that many people believe that Redbox too played a role in the downfall of Blockbuster, but by the time Redbox was created, the end was already near. Redbox was not even formed until 2002 and did not get scale until Blockbuster was already shuttering brick-and-mortar locations and looking for a suitor to help with their financial situation.

Of course, it is easy to look backward and ask the question- what was Blockbuster thinking? Why not take the Netflix deal? Again, when the Netflix co-founder flew to Dallas and proposed his deal in 2000, the Blockbuster brand was still the clear leader in the video rental industry.

The Blockbuster model was robust with thousands of retail locations, millions of customers, massive marketing budgets, and efficient operations- Blockbuster dominated the competition. In addition, Blockbuster even had leverage over the major studios. During the best years, if a studio's movie bombed at the box office, they could count on video rental revenue in thousands of Blockbuster locations to make up much of the difference of studio costs and actor salaries. See Tom Cruise, Bruce Willis, Demi Moore, and John Travolta. Listen, each of them starred in Blockbuster movies (no pun intended), but they have also had some crap movies at the theatre. No matter, those crap movies always did well on the video store rental wall.

Wielding this type of industry power, it is not surprising that the executive team at Blockbuster balked at merely handing over the brand to Netflix that they had worked so hard to build.

I will go as far as saying that Blockbuster in the 1990s had the impact Starbucks had in the 2000s. I worked for both for more than ten years each back-to-back, so I experienced the effect.

Getting a Blockbuster built in your neighborhood in the late 1980s and into the late 1990s meant that you "made it"- your community was now "on the map." That is how significant the Blockbuster brand had become.

The Blockbuster logo and storefront showed up in Hollywood movies. Hell, Blockbuster even had its own award show! That is true; there was actually a Blockbuster Awards show. The show ran for seven years from 1995 to 2001, and it attracted all the big names in movies and music. Yet another example of how significant the Blockbuster brand had become.

I attended the awards as part of recognition on two different occasions. That was one of the highlights of my time at Blockbuster.

So, with so much brand equity and ubiquity, Blockbuster seemed unstoppable. However, the Blockbuster model had a weakness that was about to be exposed. We earned an enormous amount of money by charging our customers extended viewing fees, or in layman's terms, late fees. It was silly that for years that internally, we always referred to these fees as extended viewing fees while the customers always referred to them as late fees.

Late fees had become an essential part of Blockbuster's revenue model. The ugly truth— and ultimately, the company's Achilles heel— was that its profits were highly dependent on penalizing its customers. Late fees were a shamefully high percentage of our sales mix- approximately sixteen to eighteen percent.

The irony in all of this is that Blockbuster was the one that ultimately shed light on the late fees and the economic significance of them.

In late 1999, we decided to introduce new rental terms. It would be an opportunity to demonstrate that we were a progressive brand and serve as an opportunity to finally address the late fee dilemma head-on.

There was some risk involved as our rental terms had basically been the same since the beginning of the business model fourteen years earlier. That said, perhaps even more reason that we should revisit our terms.

The cost of a movie rental at Blockbuster had also been relatively unchanged- it was always three dollars for three evenings. These terms were consistent in all company-owned stores and almost universally consistent across franchise locations. The reality is that it made sense, so there was never a need to change it.

However, if anything, you could make the case, late fees aside, that we were undercharging for renting a movie. This explains it:

In 1985, the average movie theater price in the United States was $3.55. By 1999, the average movie theater price had increased to $5.06- an increase of forty-two percent. During that same fourteen-year period, the average movie rental price at

Blockbuster had gone from $3.00 in 1985 to well, about $3.00 in 1999- no change.

So here we were, changing rental terms. In 1999, we moved to a five-day rental designed to give our customers more time to watch their movie and, in turn, that additional time could alleviate the challenge of returning the movie on time. The fact that a high number of customers that returned movies returned them on day four accruing a late fee, it seemed that this move could alleviate the pressure of mounting late fees.

That makes sense.

We also decided that we would take the rental term cost up from $3.00 to $3.99. Some stores were stair-stepped to $3.99 over a period of time, based on our pricing studies. It was the first real, broad price increase in the model since the beginning of the business and a thirty-three percent increase. This was still less than the forty-two percent uptick in movie ticket prices over that previous fourteen-year timeframe. Even with the price increase, because we decided to change the rental term from a three-day rental to a five-day rental, on a per-day basis with the extension to a five-day rental, this reduced the rental fee per day from one dollar to eighty cents, a reduction of 20%.

That makes sense.

To digress for a moment, we could have charged far more than $3.99 for a movie rental if we had appropriately positioned the experience from a marketing perspective. Think about it this way:

While the movie rental price was changed to come in line with movie theater price increases, the movie rental experience was, more often than not, a group experience. Even if the average viewing size of a movie rental at Blockbuster was two, that means that the "true" average rental price was $1.99. We could have hit people over the head with that message to demonstrate the unparalleled value in entertainment. I mean, anywhere else you go for entertainment- theme park, bowling alley, sporting events- is based on a per-person charge. I am no marketing expert, but I am an expert in common sense. Okay, back to the topic at hand.

Lastly, we decided that when a customer kept a movie beyond the due date under the new rental term (beyond five days), we would charge them a re-rental charge of $3.99.

Uh oh, that does not make sense.

The logical approach would have been to simply charge the customer a per diem on day six- either eighty cents ($3.99 divided by five days) or even one dollar per day would make sense. This would be better than a re-rental charge of $3.99, especially for customers that only kept a movie for a few hours past the five-day rental period.

That would have made sense... but that is not what we did.

There is more...

The good news is that, only a few months later, Blockbuster decided to give their customers twelve hours longer to keep their movies.

That makes sense.

This was designed to eliminate the customer's concern of racing out at midnight to return their movie. Instead, they would have until noon on day six to return the movie. We also believed that this change could take the edge off the re-rental terms storm we were still fighting from months earlier, mostly due to the re-rental charge on day six. For reasons that can be debated and were debated at the time, customers felt like they were getting twelve hours less than before... and this was after a full-on television and radio media campaign. Perhaps, the only thing more challenging than running out late at night to return a movie is attempting to do it in the middle of your workday.
Uh oh, that does not make sense.

Well, the revolution had begun for sure. With all the changes, our internal hubris said... that makes sense. For our customers, it was, uh-oh, that does not make sense.

Hubris is a funny thing. It can make you see your current situation without any fear of the future. There is such a thing as a good, healthy fear... but when hubris is in play, all things seem possible... even when they are not.

All of what I just covered is just the warm-up act. We have not even talked about the ultimatum of ultimatums yet.

But back to more of the setup.

As for our competition, Netflix had certain strengths too. By steering clear of retail locations and staying focused on a warehouse model, it lowered costs and could afford its customers far greater variety. Instead of charging to rent videos, Netflix offered subscriptions, which made annoying late fees unnecessary. Customers could watch a video for as long as they wanted or return it and get a new one. That made perfect sense to do... without the overhead of brick-and-mortar locations. Said differently, this cannot work for brick-and-mortar locations... as Blockbuster would later find out.

Netflix proved to be a very disruptive innovation to Blockbuster. It caused Blockbuster to alter its business model- and damage its profitability- to compete with the warehouse-driven model. Despite being a small, niche service at the time, Netflix had the potential to disrupt the Blockbuster business model in a way that no other business or competitor could.

However, even though the Netflix model clearly had some compelling aspects, it also had some obvious disadvantages.

Without retail locations, it was hard for people to discover it. Moreover, because its customers received their videos by mail, the service was somewhat slow and cumbersome. Waiting is not something that customers were willing to accept- even in the year 2000. In the Netflix model, people could not just pick up a movie for the night on their way home.

Still, customers loved the service, and word-of-mouth was a key contributor to growth for Netflix. I can remember working in the Blockbuster headquarters in downtown Dallas in 2002, and all the talk was about Netflix. I can recall the hallway conversations and what felt almost like peer pressure to try it out. If you did not try Netflix one time, you were ostracized... and I am only talking about Blockbuster employees! In the halls of the other floors and common areas of the building, it was clear from the chatter that other building tenants were demonstrating interest in Netflix.

Some customers were reluctant at first as they liked being able to browse movies at the store and pick one up at a moment's notice. Again, the conversations about Netflix were so pervasive that even the slow-to-adopt tried it too. They eventually fell in love with it and convinced people they knew to give it a shot. And so on and so on and so on...

While ideas usually take hold in small niches of innovators, they can often spread to early adopters, who look forward to the joy of trying something new. Once they are on board, those in the early majority begin to feel comfortable giving it a try. As each threshold is passed, the next group becomes more likely to adopt the new idea. That is how disruption happens, and that is how this disruption happened.

By the way, Netflix ultimately solved the pesky can't-get-the-movie-fast-enough-by-mail issue by consulting the former postmaster general of the United States. If one person could figure out how to do next-day delivery across the country, this was the person. Brilliant.

The irony is that Blockbuster was successful because its leadership had built a well-oiled operational machine, and Blockbuster ultimately failed because its leadership had built a well-oiled operational machine. It was a very tight network that could execute with extreme efficiency but was poorly structured to let in new information... and oh, the hubris.

In retrospect, it is not so surprising that just a few short years later, in 2004, the headlines read like this:

The Rise And Fall Of Blockbuster

The long shift finally pushed Blockbuster Inc. into bankruptcy Thursday, raising the possibility that another cultural touchstone could crumble amid the upheaval unleashed by new technology and savvy entrepreneurs who know how to exploit it.

Blockbuster's decade-long downfall from video-rental powerhouse to has-been is a story of how shortsighted management and corporate arrogance helped turn a couple of brash upstarts into the new stars of home entertainment.

Blockbuster probably would have been in a far better position had it taken a company called Netflix more seriously in 1999 when the upstart started taking DVD rental orders online and mailing the discs to people's homes.

Netflix added a twist that immediately appealed to Blockbuster customers longing for another choice: monthly subscription plans that allowed households to keep up to several DVDs at a time without incurring late fees.

The offer tapped into consumer anger because Blockbuster's late fees could double or triple the cost of a video rental. And Netflix's flat-fee system also ended up killing a golden goose for Blockbuster. In 2000, Blockbuster collected nearly $800 million in late fees, accounting for 16 percent of its revenue. Last year, those late fees had plunged to $134 million, or just three percent of its revenue.

And when Blockbuster finally launched its DVD-by-mail-and-return-to-the-store service to counter Netflix, its average revenue fell even further to just $2.79 per rental, nearly a full dollar below previous levels.

Blockbuster was the first rental service to provide billions of home videos to the masses across the country. Blockbuster made the VCR famous and built up a chain of stores that peaked at 9,100 in 2004. Now, Blockbuster was the hundred-pound weakling getting sand kicked in its face.

The company has cumulatively lost billions since 2002 and suffered the embarrassment of being taken off the New York Stock Exchange. Leading up to the bankruptcy filing, Blockbuster's market value had fallen to just $12 million, from $4 billion eight years ago.

That was literally the article that was written in 2004. Hubris.

Oh, not mentioned in the article, was the new consumer behavior called "basket-loading." I guess basket-loading became a relevant cultural term in 2002 in the manner that "streaming" became relevant in 2015. Basket-loading was what drove the average rental price down to the aforementioned $2.79 rental price. With the subscription model that Blockbuster introduced, you could rent and watch as many movies that you wanted to in a thirty-day period... and people did.

We modeled the subscription program with customers behaving the same way they were behaving in-store. We charged $19.99 per month for the subscription membership and assumed five rentals per customer per month. When customers began to average north of seven rentals per month, we were not prepared. At that point, we could not cap the rentals. If we did, we would have also capped the enthusiasm for the program. We were learning so many lessons at one time, and most of them were not good.

And one more thing to add. Let us back up a couple of years. In late 2001 at Blockbuster Video, the business was, as you would expect at that time, deteriorating. We were feeling the effects of a changing consumer, while we were not changing fast enough.

The change that we were about to make to begin 2002 was the change of all changes. If you asked a hundred people at that time what is the one thing that they would change about the video rental process, you would have likely heard two responses that surfaced as clear winners. One, I do not like driving to return the movie. Of course, that was part of the allure of Netflix. However, given that a high percentage of people rented another movie when they finished one, the return visit was not all that inconvenient, just somewhat inconvenient.

The most common answer that you would get that people wanted to change about the video rental experience... eliminate late fees!

The pesky "extended viewing fees," as we would call them at Blockbuster or as customers would call them "late fees"... and sometimes worse, were the bane of all existence in the video store business model. More often than not, customers would get no incremental benefit from late fees as it simply allowed for more time for the video to sit on their counter.

Of course, hubris says, as it is sitting on your shoulder, you can solve this problem with a few strategy meetings, a few planning sessions, and a stroke of a pen. So, we did.

Finally, to the ultimatum of ultimatums.

The End Of Late Fees

We developed a program called "The End Of Late Fees." Perhaps, we would have been better served to call it "The End Of Blockbuster" as it effectively served as the proxy for all of our self-inflicted wounds in the business during that time.

Most of the elements of "The End Of Late Fees" program were good...

... good except for the fact that late fees were ~16-18% of the total sales, and we did not exactly have a winning strategy that would ensure that we could replace that revenue.

... good except for the fact that customers that were disgruntled about the late fee haggling over the years had moved on. We clearly underestimated that we had upset many thousands of customers over the previous twenty years, arguing over what was often a two-dollar late fee. Seriously?

... good except for the fact that no rental model in American business existed without a 'late fee' component- rental car businesses, rent-to-own businesses. This would be going against the grain... a well-established grain.

Oh, and one more.

... good except for the fact that fifteen percent of the system, or about 1,000 stores, were operated by independent Blockbuster franchisees who had the ability to disagree with corporate strategy... and they did.

Other than that, "The End Of Late Fees" was good for the system. To be fair and balanced, I should take time to list all the benefits of launching it...

Okay, I am done.

Listen, the customers obviously benefitted. Rent a movie for five days and basically bring it back whenever you want. No fees. Wow! Wow... except... bringing it back when you want means people brought the movie back whenever they wanted to. Which meant that there were no movies available for anyone else to rent. The classic "solve-one-problem-and-create-another-one" scenario ensued.

I argued vehemently at the time, but obviously not loud and long enough. I argued that rental models do not work like that- i.e., car rentals, rent-to-own centers. Defined by the business model workings, there must be guardrails. Guardrail number one is that the product must be returned or paid on time or both to make a rental model work.

The theory of "The End Of Late Fees" was noble, even brilliant to a certain extent, but the idea lacked simplicity because we decided to add complexity- a classic tenet of large corporations.

Here was the problem- the press headline for "The End Of Late Fees" at Blockbuster in late 2001 read like this:

Blockbuster Inc., the nation's biggest movie-rental company, says it will eliminate late fees on games and movies as of January 1, but if you keep them too long, you buy them.

Blockbuster announced Tuesday it will continue to set due dates, with one week for games and two days or one week for movies but will give customers a one-week grace period at no additional charge, beginning New Year's Day.

"Doing away with late fees is the biggest and most important customer benefit we've ever offered in our company's history," the Blockbuster Inc. chairman and chief executive, said in a prepared statement. "So as of the first of the year, if our customers need an extra day or two with their movies and games, they can take it."

However, renters who keep the movies or games past the grace period will automatically be charged for purchasing the DVD or tape, minus the rental fee, Blockbuster said.

Customers will still be allowed to return the movie or game over the next thirty days for a refund of the purchase price but will be charged a "minimal" restocking fee, the company said.

WTF? I mean, I worked there, I was on the inside, and even I said WTF. I know what you are thinking- WTF was a thing people said in 2001?- no, not really, but I did. That is how ridiculous this was. And ultimately it was like other changes that we made in the early 2000s...
Uh oh, does not make sense.

Really? Great news, followed by, you will charge me what?

Unfortunately, it was another classic Blockbuster move... and not in a good way.

Giving the customer what they want and then ensuring that complexity was added to the mix would not be a winning formula. Customers simply no longer wanted to haggle over a two-dollar late fee- they were not asking for this change. This would become a problem, a big problem.

So, Blockbuster entered "The End Of Late Fees" change without clarity of messaging to the customer and with elements that not only seemed punitive but even more punishing than late fees. I did not believe that was possible, but we found a way to do it.

Blockbuster also entered "The End Of Late Fees" without clear alignment with franchisees. This story is not about the legality of it. That has been litigated and determined by others. While Blockbuster, as the franchisor and majority company-owned store system, had every right to do it, this was about relationships, partnerships. Others may have a different account of how we arrived at this place with our franchise community, but the one thing we can agree on is that they were collectively not happy at all with the change. After all, we were planning to blast media across television and radio airwaves.

The 'participating stores only' label works if you are a burger chain hocking toys as part of a kid's meal promoting a movie. Most parents will understand and move on to the next store to find the in-the-moment movie toy. This was not that.
We are talking about taking away late fees.

Okay, in 2020, I get that it does not mean much, especially if you are under thirty-years old. This was 2002, and this was a big freaking deal. Maybe on the scale of saying that you now get to work without having federal taxes withheld from your check. I know it is not the same thing.

The line I am drawing here is that working and taxes go together and, in 2002, so did renting movies and paying late fees. It was the American way.

All of that was about to change, and it was the ultimatum of ultimatums being presented to franchisees. Basically, get on board because this is happening, but franchisees collectively rejected the plan... if for no other reason than it felt like an ultimatum.

Some acquiesced, either because they saw the business deteriorating and thought that they might as well try something different. Others did not collect as much from late fees as a percent of business as Blockbuster corporate did based on having different rental terms, so the risk was not as significant financially. I suppose a few believed that it might actually work.

All these together represented a small percent. Many franchise owners were incensed.

Even more so after the national television ads began to run. Yes, Blockbuster blitzed the airways with commercial after commercial.

If the emotion of franchise owners tempered at any moment regarding the ultimatum, the on-air commercials only served to spike their ire, sometimes to an even higher level of discontent.

I will give Blockbuster credit for going all in. Whatever their chips were, they pushed them all to the proverbial center of the table. Metaphorically speaking, the problem is that Blockbuster was playing Poker, but the game was actually Blackjack.

I was working on the franchise side of the business at the time, and there was no way to articulate to franchisees how they could win... particularly when they did not believe that they could win.

Honestly, the only way to win was if the company could entice the millions of disgruntled renters to come back, and franchisees were not confident that would happen... and it did not happen.

Most great American brands that disappear do not disappear because of competition or technology, or other external forces. They disappear because they do not see the signs, ignore the signals due to hubris, or do not have a business intuition about seeing around the corner. The greatest culprit of business failure is usually self-inflicted wounds- ones that could have been avoided.

Listen, in the case of Blockbuster, technology would have eventually affected them to a greater degree, but who's to say that in 2020 that we would not be watching a branded streaming service called Blockbuster and renting from thousands of blue-and-gold Blockbuster kiosks.

We will never see that become a reality due to hubris and the unnecessary ultimatum that Blockbuster created that accelerated their demise.

So, what are the lessons to take away from this:

- When a significant change is coming, and you already know in advance that people are not going to like it, consider it to be an ultimatum and plan accordingly. Expect that people will be hostile. Plan for that, and you can manage anything less than hostility- like good old-fashioned anger.
- Change perceived to be an ultimatum lacks alignment somewhere along the development phase or deployment phase or likely both. The change may also lack logic. Do not assume that you developed the idea of all ideas. While it is about getting people to agree with the change, you must start by getting them to understand it.
- Ultimatums often have long-term negative implications. The impact of ultimatums often only go away with time.

Ultimatums are created- there is nothing environmental that causes them.

Finally, an ultimatum, if not immediately resolved, often invites a crisis to occur. The reality is that, at some point, you will likely face a crisis in your life. And, if you live long enough, probably many crises. And likely both personal and professional crises.

In the end, there will be enough to deal with in your life- the last thing that you should want to do, especially as a leader of people, is to create a crisis.

CHAPTER *3:*

Creating A Crisis

Creating a crisis is a technique that many have used to initiate change in their organization. In a sense, it is about manufacturing a call to action.

Creating a crisis is a niche. Here is what I mean:

Creating a crisis is not a 'Burning Platform' as there is no imminent danger. Creating a crisis is also not an ultimatum as there is no demand to do something specific.

Creating a crisis is about creating an environment of concern, resulting in an ominous atmosphere. Of course, when I describe creating a crisis in this manner, it sounds negative. That is because it is.

For creating a crisis, fear and intimidation are the pillars. Let us face it; fear and intimidation are a much easier strategy than coming up with tangible reasons for real change. However, manufacturing a crisis is something that may create other future issues to resolve, particularly when overused.

There can also be a risk that if you always create a crisis; at some point, it can lose its effectiveness. You know, the boy who cried wolf, with potentially more significant consequences.

If you are drumming up rhetoric to make it sound as though the world will end if your change isn't embraced and implemented, you will increase the risk of fracturing relationships, reduce the willingness of others to follow you, and diminish the probability of successful change in the future.

By the way, when you create a crisis in your personal life, do not be surprised when you are called a creator of drama, or worse by those around you.

In more recent years, there have been new ways to define crises or at least the result of a crisis. One approach is the New Normal.

The New Normal is a term used in many organizations, and broadly in society, introduced around the time of the 2008 Great Recession. The New Normal did drive behavioral change, but not in the manner that real, sustainable change occurs. Let me explain:

Given the economic climate of 2008,

The New Normal was about taking what was abnormal and making it commonplace.

Real, sustainable change is about taking what is commonplace and making it abnormal.

This represents the difference between forced change and real, sustainable change.

Let us explore it further: The New Normal was a seismic change to how Americans did business... in every way. After the economy began to recover, you could no longer purchase a home with zero money down. It was a complete pendulum swing where a twenty percent verifiable down payment was now needed to secure a traditional loan to purchase a home. This pushed many Americans out of the consideration set for buying a home and, in some ways, slowed the economic recovery. Okay, I am not an economist, so that is an editorial opinion.

Of course, there were many other factors, but home purchase velocity is an essential cog to the economy functioning well. That is what real economists have said.

The New Normal was also about changing interest rates- the frantic movement to keep up with the ever-changing landscape. We waited with bated breath as the Federal Reserve Chairman moved the interest rates up and down.

The New Normal was also a change in discretionary spending, a change in corporate finance behavior, and even a change in how people thought about saving money.

A new level of cynicism, almost disbelief, emerged as though our country was immune to the possibility of a recession... even though the downturn resulted from our collective, materialistic behavior.

The New Normal would serve as a foreshadow, though, in that it impacted the behavior of Millennials that saw their parents live through the crisis of 2008. Those children are now in the workforce as full-fledged adults and are behaving differently than the generation before.

There have been many articles chronicling how Millennials are much more cost-conscious and, to that point, are buying homes and cars at a slower rate than we have seen in more than fifty years. Millennials do not buy into the old ideology of the generations before them. Still, mostly, they are a bit gun-shy to purchase based on what they remember only a decade earlier- foreclosures, bankruptcies, repossessions, etc.

The New Normal was the outcome of a crisis, arguably a self- inflicted one, but for sure one that changed the country in many ways.

Some will debate whether it was avoidable or not. I do believe that greed is avoidable. I do believe that corporate finance misappropriation is avoidable. I do believe that charging those that were in need of help with the highest interest rates of all is avoidable. I am not saying that we will have a society totally free of inappropriate behavior, but I am saying that it is mostly avoidable.

We created a crisis.

The other question is whether it was bad if it caused people to change their behaviors for the better going forward- it depends. For the sake of this conversation, I will say yes, it was bad. Not just for the financial reasons and even the optics of it. More because of the forced changed that occurred as a result.

When people are forced to make changes, they may do it, but all the while doing it reluctantly and still looking for a way out. Not uncommon human behavior, but this impact was on a grand scale.

The New Normal will be talked about for generations to come. The question will be whether it is described more by the processes or by the emotions that the changes created. Based on the way that history books are crafted, I believe we know that answer.

I will digress for a moment- think about the impact of history classes if a teacher could move students to feel the stories about how our country and its culture was forged. To walk into a classroom and see high school students crying when hearing about stories of struggle. Of course, for this to occur, it would have to be different content and administrators with the ability to tell a story.

Instead, we have rather boring, straight-down-the-middle history books that most students do not remember the minute that the class ends, and the school year is over. I admit this is also a total editorial view. Perhaps, my expectations of the educational system are too high.

Okay, back to the topic. Getting to the root cause is important in understanding a crisis, and with that, you ultimately must give people a reason to believe in the need for change and that something different must happen to end a crisis.

I bet that when you began reading this chapter, and I mentioned the New Normal, you thought I would talk about the coronavirus crisis.

I did not, and I did not to make a point. But I will now.

Everyone loves a good catchphrase, and here comes the New Normal all over again in 2020 as if no one has ever said it before. The same things that were said about 2008 could be said about 2020. I know these two crises are not remotely the same. I agree, and yet here we are using the same language- the New Normal.

The New Normal was about taking what was abnormal and making it commonplace.

Is this what we really want now in 2021? Do we really want to wear facemasks until the end of time? Surely not.

This is why the correlation between change and crises is so important. Real, sustainable change is about you dictating what happens, not allowing yourself to have things dictated to you.

The good news is that we had the ability from the very beginning of the coronavirus crisis to determine how it would go- we had control. However, that also meant that the only way that we could control it is that humankind had to do its part- be responsible, take it seriously, be courteous and thoughtful of others, leaders had to role model what to do. Well, we know how that all turned out.

As I was sharing the formation of this chapter, someone asked me whether I believe that the coronavirus crisis was created. I said yes, I do, but not in the way you are thinking. Let me explain:

For me, this is not about whether it was created in a lab in Wuhan, created by the democrats, created by someone to eradicate a part of our population, and all the other conspiracy theories. I cannot go there. We are where we are.

What I am speaking to is the inability, or better said, unwillingness, for people to change. The refusal to take measures to keep themselves safe... and others. The reluctance to sacrifice for the greater good. Okay, I am lecturing too much on this.

What I am trying to say is this:
Change is a choice- I will get to that later in the book.

The takeaway here with the New Normal is that human beings work in cycles. We have a desire, at times, to label everything. I am not sure that doing that helps us- marking each of these periods post-recovery as The New Normal or maybe worse, the sequel that I have heard, the Next Normal. Both are stupid-ass terms- I prefer to spend my time and energy on fixing the problem and capturing key learnings so that it does not happen again.

In both situations, the signs of a crisis were always there... and we did not respond to them.

Another significant crisis that we faced was 9/11.

With all the tragedy that came with September 11, 2001, the entire country has been on edge for a long time, and understandably so. My condolences to those who lost loved ones or knew those who did lose people close to them during this tragedy.

To be clear, 9/11 itself was not a created crisis- it was an attack on our livelihood, our democracy.

However, there were offspring activities that could be an example of creating a crisis.

I recognize that discussing 9/11 is a sensitive subject, but I am going to go there anyway. I believe that everything we experience can and should have a post-mortem process that forces us to reflect on what happened, why it happened, what we learned from it, and how we prevent it from happening again.

These are fundamental questions, but I also believe that they are basic responsibilities. So, let us discuss one crisis aspect of 9/11.

The color-coded terror threat system is one of them. It may have been difficult for any of us to look at the process objectively as it was put in place. Honestly, most of us were less than rational at that time- we were hurting as a country, and we were uncertain about the future. Fast-forward almost twenty years now and let us examine it:

As many of you may recall, as a result of 9/11, the government decided to implement the color-coded terror threat levels. Inspired by the forest fire color system's success, the scale consisted of five color-coded threat levels intended to reflect the probability of a terrorist attack and its potential gravity. The five threat levels were:

> Severe (red) severe risk
> High (orange) high risk
> Elevated (yellow) significant risk
> Guarded (blue) general risk
> Low (green) low risk

Once implemented in the aftermath of 9/11, it was a check-in every day. We were riveted, watching the news waiting for the next threat level change. What discovery had our intelligence community made this time that would alert us to the progress being made in the War On Terror? This threat level change went on for weeks... then months... then years.

There came a point, not immediately and not all Americans at the same time, but over time, that we became cynical about the terror threat levels. I mean, the threat level was at elevated (yellow) significant risk for most of its time in existence- for more than two and a half years. It was raised to high (orange) high risk six times during that period only to be dropped back down.

The specific government actions triggering the different threat level changes were not always revealed to the public, adding to the cynicism.

As a result of the threat level system, actions were taken, including increasing police and other security presence at landmarks and other high-profile targets, closer monitoring of international borders and other points of entry, ensuring that emergency response personnel were ready, and, in some cases, even deploying the National Guard.

However, there was never a point when information was published and made available to the public, and thus no way to tell whether the current threat level was accurate or no way to justify the move. Interestingly, the threat levels Green (low risk) and Blue (general risk) were never even used. The threats that caused the threat levels to change and the sources were seldom revealed.

However, supporters of the system defended this approach by stating that providing detailed, current intelligence about terror organizations would endanger the ability to gather similar information in the future. Whether that was true or not, it began to create a fracture in the trust of the American public.

It is hard to go back in time to remember how you felt—understandably, many of you do not want to remember how you felt, and some of you are not old enough to remember. In some ways, it was insult to injury. What do I mean by that? The color threat levels appeared to be creating a crisis in reaction to the crisis that occurred.

Acting on intelligence information and keeping it from the American people is indeed a matter of national security. Using intelligence, intentionally or not, to heighten the fears of the American people is arguably creating a crisis.

Creating a crisis does not happen only in government or in our economy; it also occurs in business.

As is often said, imitation is the greatest form of flattery, and many U.S. companies have looked at the Toyota Production model, specifically Lean Principles, as the gold standard of productivity.

As described in one definition, Lean Principles refer to a technique developed to minimize process waste and maximize the value of the product or service to the customer, without compromising the quality.

Additionally, Lean is an approach to running an organization to improve products, services, or processes by which consumers do not pay for mistakes or waste. Instead, they pay for value. Lean uses methods for eliminating factors that waste time, effort, or money by analyzing a business process and then cutting out any steps that do not create value for consumers.

I worked for an organization that attempted to implement elements of Toyota- the Toyota Production System, specifically Lean Principles.

Let me disclaim this by saying that I love the people there, and principally, those responsible for Lean have long since left the organization. Now is a good time to tell this story from almost a decade ago.

During that time, I was working in a broad leadership role responsible for hundreds of stores. The Lean Principles were introduced as a set of tools to assist in the identification and steady elimination of waste. As waste is eliminated, quality improves while production time and costs are reduced. Lean was also focused on saving time, eliminating unnecessary motion, and designed to address executing repetitive activities with a repetitive approach.

One of the most significant opportunities identified for improvement at the time was beverage production, which led to the development of a set of processes called Beverage Routine. Considering that it was primarily a beverage business, the sheer disproportionate amount of labor hours spent on this activity made it necessary to focus there. Saving any number of seconds could be extrapolated into millions of dollars annually.

Other ideas that were introduced in the suite of tools were activities like "Spaghetti Mapping" - a process of diagramming customer or employee movement and exercises to expose inefficiency opportunities. Watching the patterns of actions and tracking the actual usage and steps along the way would provide clues as to what could be changed.

The "spaghetti map" was exclusive to each store's flow of customers, and it informed problems that needed to be solved in that specific store. This was an excellent tool, my favorite of all the tools that were introduced. The "spaghetti map" was perhaps even underutilized in the scope of all the tools.

I found myself drawn to this tool because it was a reaction to how customers behave in their interaction with the brand. When you make life easier for the customer, life usually gets better for the business. The insight that it gave us allowed us to make changes relevant to each store.

There was also the "Go-See" approach to watch what happens in the store and then look to solve problems that are found that will improve the customer experience and improve the work experience of the employees. The "Go-See" proved to be a powerful tool during the peak times of the store and for observing customer behavior in the drive-thru channel of the business.

There were many incredible ideas and process improvements that spawned from Lean. In part because an element of the learning was solving problems where the work happens.

Lean was influential in many ways, and one of the very few processes that I saw over the years that worked and sustained.

However, there were challenges, and this is where change management has to be thoroughly vetted for clarity, alignment, acceptance, and logic.

All of the elements of Lean were great, except I did not work for any companies, including this one, that was involved with assembly line work or manufacturing work. I have worked in retail for thirty-six years- all brick and mortar stores with customer-facing storefronts. What I know to be true is that the customer comes first. Period. This is not the same as the customer is always right. This is about giving the customer priority over tasks. There are no exceptions to that. Of course, you can make exceptions at the risk of losing sales. I would like to hear the argument for that approach.

Lean was particularly important for process improvement,

and the effort to implement it was all with incredibly good intentions. It served to pull up those who lacked experience, organization, or problem-solving skills in their leadership roles. That is important for me to acknowledge, personally knowing many of the leaders that worked tirelessly to implement Lean.

However, change management does not reward effort- it rewards precision, transparency. Change management rewards ideas that embrace what people want and need. Change management rewards logic.

So back to my initial point in this book. Change is not a process... change is an emotion. However, Lean was all process.

The number of resources dedicated to introducing Lean was impressive... and for the context of this story, that is not a compliment.

There were full corporate teams, coaches in the field, all field leaders with some level of implementation responsibility, and ultimately an almost cult-like approach to implementing it. Yes, I am using the term cult-like in this context... for a reason. Lean was no typical rollout, and the only option was to get on board and evangelize Lean. Any speaking against it would not be tolerated.

We had brought in a leader from outside the organization to lead this process, and unfortunately, he did not know anything about our company. That is okay; it would be unfair to expect anyone to come from the outside and be knowledgeable right away. The more significant concern is that he did not know anything about leadership- that was the gap.

However, I am not putting this all on the new leader coming in; we should have known better internally. I will come back to that.

By the way, the company at the time was delivering mid to high single-digit comps, record EBITDA growth, and opening stores at a pace that any U.S. company would celebrate.

Nonetheless, something had to be wrong- a crisis had to be created. The signals were that we would lose our way if we did not implement Lean.

I am sure some of you are reading this and possibly believing that I am being melodramatic. Also, my telling of this story may sound harsh to some of you- some that remember it. Yes, my approach to telling this story is intentionally crude. I believe firmly in disclosing the part of the story that does not get shared or does not get considered. After all, the consensus view typically overruns the belief that most people may independently have. Like the media, if you hear something a thousand times, you may begin to believe it, whether it is true or not.

This is important because change should not feel forced, and it should not be forced. Change must be developed, introduced, and implemented in a way that inspires people to want to make the change. Anything short of that is not a complete success.

Back to Lean.
For those of you reading this that lived through the Lean

implementation, you will get this. For those of you that did not live through it, you can apply the story to any change that you have been force-fed in your leadership role.

So off we went. Clearly, something was wrong in the system for Lean to come along and be necessary to our future existence... and I am not joking about the importance placed on this initiative.

We had Created A Crisis.

So, the rest of the story.
Lean was implemented over the next year, and no other initiative would knock it off the track. That was surprising considering how many new initiatives pop up throughout the year that are not on the original operating plan or strategic plan and the interruption they usually create- not with Lean. Lean was forced through- all the activities were completed, and processes embedded- that box could be checked.

Earlier in the chapter, I mentioned that there were challenges, and this is where change management has to be thoroughly vetted for logic, clarity, alignment, and acceptance. Well, let us start first with logic.

At times, Lean did not pass the logic test. We had top-level store managers across the country who had their successes reduced by the rigidity of Lean. Some store managers lost sales and profits due to being required to abandon what was already working to allow for the Lean implementation. It is the equivalent of wanting to change the incorrect form of an athlete who is already best in the world at what they do. It is hard to make a case for doing that.

I love conformity as much as the next person; however, the lack of logic impacted our customers- clearly by their vote to spend less money as sales were declining in some of our best stores.

This is where clarity comes in. Managers want to ensure that what they are doing is meeting the right objective, which most managers believed was to gain efficiencies, reduce waste, and improve the lives of the employee and the customer. There was a conflict at times as the customer seemed to get squeezed at the expense of embedding the processes. The tension between the "assembly line" work mentality of Lean and the ever-changing reality of moment-to-moment changes in a restaurant was at odds.

Alignment was not a team sport when it came to Lean. To be fair, alignment is incredibly challenging to achieve on a large-scale project implementation. However, it was predetermined that this was going to work...even if it did not. Again, the processes ruled.

Finally, we get to acceptance. I do not recall the question being asked if anyone agreed with Lean. This was not that kind of rollout- everyone was expected to be on board. Of course, not everyone was, but you would have never known it. Again, the processes ruled.

In the end, the processes were such a focus that something interesting happened.

The processes became the initiative. The processes became the change.

This is where we should have known better. The new leader clearly had carte blanche to roll this out, but that was one voice. This is where the internal voices needed to emerge. What I mean- well, let me share an experience:

As a regional vice-president, I spent time out in multiple markets, in hundreds of stores, watching these new processes for months. This was not only a priority for employees in the stores to do but also for the district managers and regional directors. Even though these positions did not work in the stores, this became their priority as well as folding tee-shirts. Folding tee-shirts? I will come back to that.

Well, two things here with this statement about process that I need to stop and address.

One, I fundamentally believe in role clarity and role separation in business. Allow me to use a sports analogy to support this point: **Coaches coach, and players play.**

In sports, a coach stands on the sideline, calls the plays, and attempts to inspire their team to out-execute the other team. A coach cannot go on the field to play, no matter how frustrated they may be with their team's performance.

Players execute the play and take direction from their coach. It is not commonplace or an expectation for players to go to the sideline or bench and provide coaching to the coach- that usually does not turn out so well.

The roles are apparent. In a multi-unit retail structure, I do not believe it should be any different. The "coaches" are the district managers, regional directors, regional vice-presidents, in my example, or the equivalent roles in the organization for which you work.

The "players" are the store managers, general managers, unit managers, and their teams. Of course, the playing field for this analogy is inside of the four walls of the store.

I submit that it is not critical for the coach to be able to execute the play... or fold tee-shirts. To further this point, some of the most successful coaches in sports were not superstars, and some did not even play their sport at the highest level.

Exhibit A- John Madden in football. An entire video game franchise named after him, and Madden revered as one of the greatest football coaches and football minds of all time... and he never played a single play in the NFL. He simply knew how to coach and inspire people at the highest level.

Now, to the tee-shirts. I know that I mentioned that this was a beverage business, so what do folding tee-shirts have to do with this business? Nothing, but part of embedding processes, were activities taught from the regional vice presidents on down, including a folding tee-shirt example to help explain the approach. I am not making this up.

Every region office pulled all the regional directors and regional vice-presidents from across the country together to go through an exercise on folding tee-shirts. It was meant to teach a lesson about repeatable routines... to a group that would never be behind the counter to execute the repeatable routines- see coaches and players example.

Oh, and there was a Mr. Potato Head involved. Honestly, I do not even remember exactly what that was all about. I believe it had to do with what order we took him apart and put him back together.

I am not attempting to be funny regarding this. It was not funny at all. It was hours and hours away from doing the job we were supposed to be doing- inspiring and leading people and delivering business results.

Okay, now to the second point. When it comes to observation, it is crucial to ensure that you observe what is relevant and what matters, or you will find yourself solving a problem that you did not intend to or worse, solving a problem that does not even exist. You will hear more about solving for solutions later in the book.

In all my observations, some stood out more than others. Some observations were so egregious that the leaders watching the beverage routine process would literally sit with their back to the storefront and, ultimately, with their back to the customers. This was fascinating... and disappointing. This is where logic needed to enter the equation.

The field teams were so good at Beverage Routine activities focused on watching employees that no one was watching the customer.

It was a seminal moment.

There were a lot of great aspects of Lean than moved the entire system of stores forward. For all the good, though, there was a lack of balance. It was a one-sided, one-dimensional approach that did not get the proper push back that change requires in the development phase and certainly not during the implementation phase. Just because something is not wrong does not mean that it is right, or entirely right.

Lean did not always put the customer first.

Lean actually slowed down some of the best store managers. This is another point where logic needed to enter the equation.

Ultimately, Lean did not always consider the emotional aspect of change. Processes ruled the day.

The point of this story is not about a company implementing poor processes. The point is about losing sight of what is most important and distracting yourself from doing the hard, necessary, basic work of taking care of the customer and delivering good operations. It is not uncommon to see large matrix organizations find a project to 'show' that something was being done. Often, just going and doing the work, the basic blocking-and-tackling will be fine... and it will save you money.

So, when consultants show up in your building, listen closely to their conversations. See if they know what they are talking about. Find out early if there is a risk that they will wreck your business.

Consultants are just ordinary people who know a lot about a specific topic and perhaps nothing about many other topics. In the end, they do want to be helpful. I should know as I have been one of them.

If consultants do not ask you questions, give them answers anyways. Answers that they do not know that they need. Depending on their level of hubris, they may or may not thank you later. This is what I do know:

When the project names start flying around in the halls and boardrooms of your organization, ask questions. When project names lose the project prefix, be concerned, and ask even more questions.

At that point, it is likely that the consultants are under contract and will be around for a while. Or worse, as in the example with Lean, they get hired as an employee!

It is possible that a crisis is being created.

When a crisis occurs, and it is resolved, it is important to capture key learnings to better prepare when the next crisis comes along or worse, when you create another one.

I admit that my storytelling has a bias slant to it. Of course, I recognize it and own it because, in this example, I lived through it.

I am sure you have your biases as well. We often call these preferences or pet peeves or... anything but biases.

Bias is such a strong word. Let us talk about it and its impact on the change process.

CHAPTER 4:

Bias Is A Four-Letter Word

If you grew up as I did, you might be familiar with the term "four-letter word." While the term four-letter word is typically associated with coarse or offensive language, many four-letter words show up in organizations that are not explicit, but that can be damaging. In every book, I will dedicate a chapter to a four-letter word.

In this book, that word is bias. Of course, there are four letters in this word, but that is not why I am talking about bias. I am discussing bias because it is a little word that can derail your business or personal life. Bias is basically the lens through which we see the world.

I will start with this: I have plenty of biases of my own. However, I want to believe that I am more liberal and objective than the next person and that I can accept new information without judgment. I am certain that I am not certain that is true, although I want it to be. The only way to not have biases is not to have any knowledge of anything or experiences with anything. Of course, for that to occur, we would not be a living human being. Every single experience that we have contributes to our bias portfolio. It is then strengthened by the things that we believe in, that are agreeable to us and rarely weakened by those things that we do not believe in- called contrary information.

Case in point, let us talk about politics. If you believe that you are an "independent voter," which more than half of the U.S. population identifies themselves as, watch CNN and Fox News and see which one you spend the entire day nodding your head to or shaking your head at most often. Either way, you will know what your "true" political party is. If you can watch both without any emotional reaction, then you are probably a real independent or a robot. I would submit that is an exceedingly small part of our population, being a real independent that is.

When contrary evidence is presented, we learn about our biases... or ignore them- which is usually easier. Taking the time to investigate contrary information is responsible... but it does not feel good. It means that you have to face your realities about what you believe to be true that, in fact, may not be true.

Bias is disproportionate weight in favor of or against an idea or thing, usually in a closed-minded, prejudicial, or unfair way. Biases can be innate or learned.

In recent years, the term unconscious bias has moved into the lexicon of the workplace. Unconscious biases are learned stereotypes that are automatic, unintentional, deeply engrained, universal, and able to influence behavior. I will come back to this later in the chapter.

Bias is a very wide-ranging topic, so I will not attempt to broadly take it on. Instead, I want to focus on deep-seated bias. Bias that is so embedded that you could be presented with contrary information that is proven or factual, and you still reject it.

You may be saying, what does bias have to do with change? Bias can prevent us from seeing information as it is; instead, we see it through our own lens, based on our own experiences. That change of view can change the change you are presented with (intentional alliteration), so bias is material to the conversation of change. If you believe so strongly in what you are currently doing, you will not likely be open to change, even if it is proven to be better for you.

Change is hard enough to implement. If biases prevent you from getting the message through to those going through the change, they could be interpreting it incorrectly or, worse, be a complete no-go on the change.

One aspect of life where people can have strong biases is regarding celebrities. People that we all believe that we know because the person has created an image that we either like or dislike. That is then perpetuated by our perceived frequent access to the person and their life and how we hear others discuss them. We have formed a deep-seated bias, which can be positive or negative.

I will digress for a moment to share an example of such bias. I often reference sports to make a point. When I do so, I am not assuming that everyone follows sports. Instead, for this point, I use sports because of the deep-seated emotions that come with competition- cheering for your favorite team or player or against another team or player. Also, a sport leaves us with fewer gray areas than most aspects of our lives. In sports, there is a scoreboard- there is a clear winner and a clear loser. This conversation is not about winning and losing, though. It is about being able to point to something finite, definitive.

So, with sports generating so much emotion, let us discuss someone that has been at the center of that emotion over the past twenty years.

My example here is Barry Bonds, former baseball player and all-time leader in home runs. By sharing this perspective, I submit this disclaimer- I am not attempting to change your view of Barry Bonds, only ensure that you hear the perspective that is rarely represented.

By most accounts, there is a negative bias related to Barry Bonds, and that is that Bonds was and still is a villain in the baseball world. Bonds is primarily considered the poster boy for the steroid era.

During his playing days, Bonds was surly, angry, selfish, entitled, ungrateful, combative, rude, and obnoxious... and those were some of the more flattering adjectives used to describe him.

He allegedly used steroids and cheated his way to the home run record. Bonds played with a chip on his shoulder. He was short with reporters in post-game interviews. Most of the media and even the commissioner of baseball at the time did not like Bonds. The commissioner stood in the stands and turned his back to the field in protest when Bonds hit the record-breaking 756th home run. I am not sure how that was even allowed, given that the commissioner is supposed to be impartial.

Oh well, all of this played into the negative narrative about Barry Bonds... and almost everyone bought into it.

By the way, Barry Bonds, post-baseball career, has acknowledged all of this. He said that he even attempted to change this persona while playing, but he ultimately felt like the negative vortex he had already created was too strong to change. Now, I am not sure that I am buying that, but those are his words, and who am I to say what his true intentions were.

However, the other side of the Barry Bonds narrative, not necessarily positive, just factual, is this:

Barry Bonds had arguably the most remarkable baseball pedigree of any player in history, mitigating the need to even use steroids- here is why:

Barry Bond's father, Bobby Bonds, was an incredible major league baseball player. He was considered one of the first five-tool players- a term used to describe a player that could hit, hit for power, run, catch, and throw and do all five at a high level. Bobby played fourteen seasons and was only the second player in the history of baseball at that time with at least 300 career home runs and 300 stolen bases. The only other player in history to do that was Willie Mays, who is regarded by most to be one of the top players of all time. Bobby played alongside Willie Mays in San Francisco for six seasons, and some following baseball at the time even felt that Bobby was better than Willie.

Bobby Bonds had his own demons, one of them being cocaine. His career was cut short, and frankly, it was not as memorable overall as it could have been. This is important context as many people may not even know that Barry Bonds had a father that played baseball and at a high level. Even with the drug addiction, Bobby had cast such a massive shadow of his own as a baseball player that Barry Bonds was commonly called Bobby during his first few seasons and referred to as Bobby's son.

Second, Barry Bonds' godfather was Willie Mays. Willie shared everything that he knew about the game with young Barry. Willie Mays was also considered a five-tool player, so every aspect of the game was an opportunity for Barry to learn from one of the greatest of all time. When Willie Mays retired, he was third on the all-time home run list, trailing only Babe Ruth and Hank Aaron.

Third, Barry Bonds' cousin was Hall of Fame slugger Reggie Jackson. Jackson hit 563 home runs and was sixth all-time in home runs when he retired from baseball.

Jackson played with a similar brash, chip-on-his-shoulder style that drew the ire of his contemporaries. However, right or wrong, Jackson got away with his behavior, frankly because he backed up his bravado on the field with his performance. Jackson is still revered for one of the most memorable baseball moments of all time- hitting three home runs in a World Series game in 1977.

The most remarkable aspect of this performance, other than it being on the biggest stage of baseball, is that Jackson hit three home runs in a row off three consecutive pitches from three different pitchers. It earned him the nickname "Mr. October"- arguably the greatest compliment there is in baseball.

So, between inheriting genes from an all-star father and hall of fame cousin and learning from one of the greatest of all time, Barry Bonds was destined to be great, truly great. There is no one else in the history of the game that has a pedigree that approaches this. Barry Bonds was a blend of talent, knowledge, hard work, and perhaps steroids at some point in time.

Barry Bonds won a record seven Most Valuable Player awards and had won three in his first eight seasons. Notably, the first eight seasons were never in question about steroid use. Most baseball experts would put Bonds in the Hall of Fame based on those years before the steroid controversy because of how compelling his career statistics were already.

So, let me summarize this and get to the relevance related to deep-seated bias and change management.

First, Bonds has all but admitted post-career that he was a jerk. However, being a jerk is not a crime- my words, not his. Because of the personal disdain that Bonds created with his persona and the cloud of suspicion of steroid use, the narrative about Bonds that was always portrayed was one-sided... villain.

The perspective here is that if you already knew all of this about Barry Bonds and disliked him, then so be it. If you did not know this information, does it now change your view of Barry Bonds? I would assume that the answer for most people is- not likely. Back to my point earlier, deep-seated bias is often not erased with a singular presentation of contrary information.

This is a form of bias. We form opinions based on indirect stimuli or said differently, second-hand information. That is not all that uncommon, but the distinction here is that for it to become deep-seated biases, it is likely that we have only heard one-sided information, exclusively... and for a long time.

For many of us, we may not be aware that bias is getting in our way when attempting to change some aspect of our life.

So, where does deep-seated bias begin? Well, of course, with our parents. By definition, something can only become 'deep-seated' by information being presented in one of two ways- one, as a steady drumbeat, each time getting embedded deeper and deeper into the psyche or two, being presented less often, but in such an overt way that it becomes deeply entrenched quickly. So, what do I mean?

Let us start with the biases that are presented with a steady drumbeat.

Whether it occurs in the household or out in public, what children see or hear over and over again is going to inform them of what is 'good' or 'bad.' By the way, this is not about whether the parent is doing it intentionally or not- that would allow for excuses, and I do not want to entertain that for this conversation. I only want to talk about the outcomes, the impact.

So, the parental conditioning begins by activities such as what channels the parent watches, what flags or signs that they put in their yard, what stickers they place on their vehicles, what church they decide to attend and drag their children along to, their personal view of the military and oh, what words they use to describe other people different than them.

Again, I am not here to judge whether it is intentional. These are things that real parents are doing every day.

The point is that our children are listening and watching and filing it all away... usually as early as the age of three. They are forming biases or said differently; we are creating biases on their behalf.

By the time we enter adulthood, we are literally spending as much time questioning our own biases as we are learning about the broader world around us. So many things that we experience as adults may be in conflict with what we had been told for the first eighteen years or so. It is not all bad; that is not the point here. The point is that it may be different.

Let us now talk about biases that are presented overtly. These deep-seated biases can literally form from one-time events. For example:

If you witnessed a loved one shot and killed by the police, you might have a deep-seated bias against law enforcement for the rest of your life. No matter what other good deeds are done by other police officers, this one event is so traumatic that there may be nothing that can change that feeling. In a situation like this, we may be party to hearing someone share a disdain for law enforcement without knowing their backstory. This is where life situations and our biases collide. Someone who is married to an officer that hears this conversation, or perhaps has lost a sibling in the line of fire, would likely have a visceral reaction to someone who dislikes police officers. Neither person is right or wrong- their experiences shape their biases.

Another example- if you are involved in a car accident, and the cause of the crash was a failure in the brake system, you may no longer trust that car manufacturer. Because of that, you never purchase another car from that automaker for the rest of your life. Even if there had been a recall on the vehicle due to a defect with the braking system and you failed to take your vehicle in when alerted, you may still hold the automaker emotionally accountable.

These are one-time events that leave such an indelible mark that no contrary evidence presented going forward may change your view.

Now, back to unconscious bias.

A good friend of mine has been a student of unconscious bias. I have listened to him talk about this topic for years and found it interesting. I never really connected it to the change process until I began writing this book... and then it hit me. There are barriers, deep-seated barriers that people have that creep into the workplace and have nothing to do with the organization or even their leaders.

The relevant point here is not only do the leaders not detect the unconscious biases, but even the employee does not, thus the reason this term was born. Many of our reactions, mostly the visceral ones, are related to these deep-seated biases that we have developed.

Unconscious bias can create an impenetrable barrier. Yes, I know, that is a tautology.

For example, a useful awareness activity for unconscious bias training taken from the social psychological literature is the Father and Son activity, adapted from Pendry, Driscoll, & Field in 2007. In this activity, participants are instructed to solve the following problem:

A father and son were involved in a car accident in which the father was killed, and the son was seriously injured. The father was pronounced dead at the scene of the accident. The son was taken by ambulance to a nearby hospital and was immediately wheeled into the operating room. A surgeon was called. Upon arrival and seeing the patient, the attending surgeon exclaimed, "Oh my gosh, I cannot operate on him, he's my son!" Can you explain this?

More than half of the participants who are faced with this challenge do not think of the most logical answer: the surgeon is the boy's mother. Instead, many participants invent elaborate stories such as the boy was adopted, the boy had two fathers, the surgeon was his natural father, or the father in the car was a priest.

As such, the exercise illustrates the power of automatic, stereotyped associations. For some individuals, the assumption of all surgeons being men is so strong that it interferes with problem-solving and making accurate judgments. Most people who make this assumption are often embarrassed that they could not solve the problem instead of focusing on this bias. The good news is that now when this situation is presented to a group, they are more likely to get to the conclusion of the mother being a surgeon than in 2007. That is progress, I suppose.

Now, back to the change process. Unconscious bias is, in part, what keeps us from accepting new information. For the sake of this conversation:

Unconscious bias keeps us from automatically saying yes to change.

There is something there that tells us this change is not agreeable to us, and yet there are occasions in which we cannot even articulate why.

Let us get further into bias related to change. Indeed, an offshoot of deep-seated bias is the eight-word questions that I raised earlier in the book:

> "This is the way it's always been done."
> "Things are fine the way that they are."
> "If it is not broke, don't fix it."
> "We tried that before, and it didn't work."

These are statements of resistance. The reality is that resistance is part of the change process. Still, these statements almost assure that you will get resistance as the leader or that others will demonstrate opposition as the recipient of change.

There are times in our lives that we have heard something so often and for so long that it has to be true. Even when it is not true and is refuted with evidence, we may still be confused, attempting to reconcile the new information against the pile of information we have been carrying around for so long.

So, how should you handle these deep-seated biases when they show up during the change process? I will answer that question by simply stating... carefully.

Ignoring or minimizing deep-seated bias is a dangerous proposition. Even if you dismiss someone's personal deep-seated bias as ridiculous, you have a different responsibility of discipline as a leader to listen and find a way forward that gets done what you want and what the employee needs.

There is one more part of bias to explore that I mentioned earlier in the book. Covering, or sometimes described as identity covering. Identity covering in the workplace has implications for diversity and inclusion initiatives. It also has an impact as it relates to change. Let me explain, but first, let us talk about what identity covering is.

Identity covering is the act of concealing something about oneself to avoid making other people feel uncomfortable or simply avoid being judged by others because of a specific characteristic about you. It is about downplaying your identity elements, such as race, religion, gender, disability, or sexual orientation, to avoid feelings of anxiety, frustration, fear, discrimination, or harassment.

While it may not seem significant to work performance or productivity, researchers have determined quite the opposite. Identity covering in the workplace can have detrimental effects on things like the amount of energy available to commit to workplace tasks. This might happen because many employees' energy is devoted to concealing a personal characteristic or feelings of isolation. If employees do not feel free to be themselves around their colleagues, they may not be as effective.

So, what exactly do I mean by this? Here are a couple of examples:

A few years ago, I worked with a leader that was doing great work in his role and was often praised by the organization. However, he was covering. The only way that I could describe his dilemma was that he was "hiding in plain sight." He was a gay man, and no one knew it. For the select few in his personal life that did know, he did not feel judged by them or even fearful that his secret would get out.

I can recall us having a couple of conversations about it, and he was certain that, if exposed, he would be limited in his promotional abilities within the company. Now, you could look at that and say that it is more of a discrimination issue. It could be, but what I know for sure is that it is identity covering.

Specific situations presented themselves, which resulted in his need to cover his identity. For example, he felt like he could not bring his partner to the company Christmas party or other functions. For an employee with nothing to "cover," this internal struggle does not exist.

Other examples: A practicing Muslim going to his car on his lunch break to pray to avoid being noticed by co-workers. A working mom not keeping photos of her kids at her desk so that she appears more career-driven.

Again, those that have nothing to 'cover' are likely not aware of the lengths that employees around them are going to just to keep their secrets. Their insecurity may not be an issue with anyone around them, but they have made themselves believe that it is, that it definitely is.

According to the report Uncovering Talent, from the Deloitte University Leadership Center for Inclusion, more than sixty percent of workers in the workforce today demonstrate some form of activity defined as identity covering.

All this is relevant to change. Just as someone that does not get a job may believe that the reason for rejection had to do with their gender or race, a person who is covering may feel that their identity issue is holding them back.

As it relates to change, it can put your people in a defensive position when the change is presented. They may believe that the change is meant to create a disadvantage for them in some way based on the element of their life that they have been covering.

For example, the leader of a team may decide that the weekly meeting held in their store needs to move from 10:00 am on Saturdays to 10:00 am on Sundays. The reason for the move is that Saturdays are too busy, and it makes it more challenging to hold the meeting and still schedule enough people to work on the same day to handle the volume of business. However, someone on the team may believe that they are being penalized because they have always had Sundays off, which they requested under the guise of coaching soccer.

Moving the meeting to Sunday seems like a logical thing to do, but for that employee who practices their religion on Sundays, it may feel like it was done to spite them... even though no one knows about their religion. The person may even go as far as to believe they are intentionally discriminated against because of their religion. Meanwhile, that has never crossed your mind as the person leading the change as you are not even aware of their self-imposed dilemma.

Another example is a leader that wants to do something fun and post pictures of their staff from grade school. On the team is a transgender employee that no one is aware of. This employee would have to share a picture that would be obvious in exposing what they have been covering. Again, most people would never have to worry about something like this, but this employee could feel like the activity is meant to expose their past.

Bias can be a huge barrier to change. It can also be invisible during the change process, so having something so impactful that you cannot even detect is difficult for a leader to handle.

Perhaps, the only thing more difficult to detect than bias when going through the change process is when people are not saying anything at all.

This becomes the responsibility of the leader to identify the quiet voices.

CHAPTER 5:

The Quiet Voices

While most of this book focuses on the hostility of change- the obvious, visual, verbal, emotional resistance to change, there is another side.

There are the quiet voices. The ones that do not ever get noticed- mostly because they do not want to be noticed.

The quiet voices may be doing severe damage to your change management process. This is the sabotage I referenced earlier in the book.

Detecting the quiet voices takes authentic, compassionate leadership. It is more than skill; it is more than intuition, it is more than investing time, it is more than caring- it is all of this.

There are two sides to this. The quiet voices can also be positive- a catalyst for change, an ally. Here is what I mean: the quiet voices often have answers.

The least likely person in a room of people to raise their hand is possibly the person with the greatest understanding and, potentially, the greatest acceptance of the change. This person has spent so much time listening and being introspective that they are likely digesting more information and accepting the change quicker than others.

As important, they are not sitting there, spending time thinking of what they will say next in the conversation. When a person is composing their following response in a conversation before the other person finishes speaking, their ability to listen and process is diminished.

In this chapter, I want to strike a balance between good and evil when it comes to the quiet voices, but let us start with where it is detrimental to the process:

On the challenging side, I believe that there are three levels of quiet voices:

The saboteur, the dissenter, and the silent assassin.

The Saboteur

In the preface of the book, I referenced that change can invoke a passively hostile resistance, often difficult to detect, but just as detrimental to the change process you are attempting to implement as the obvious resistance.

Because this can be difficult to detect, it requires you to be curious to seek out who is attempting to derail the change and trying to do it without anyone knowing.

The saboteur knows what they are doing but does not want others to know. They may be motivated by the need to minimize their own losses. They are unlikely to infect others directly because they are not being open about what they are doing, but their behavior may still influence others.

Staying anonymous is their key to success. Planting the seeds of doubt into the change process in such a subtle way that no one notices.

However, if you listen and observe, there will be signs:

The saboteur will ask leading-the-witness type questions. For example, "Have we tested this change somewhere to work through all the potential problems?" That seems like an innocent enough question... it is probably not. The question is asked with a negative slant to plant the seeds of doubt. It is an inference that the change has a flaw, and if it is not discovered soon, we could all be doomed as a result of the impending change.

To go further, the saboteur will ask the types of questions with the belief that they can 'save the day' for everyone else. Almost to the point of expecting to get credit for coming up with the tough question that no one else thought about. I recognize that most people may not think this way, but if you are leading change, you have to spot this.

I promise you that I am not a conspiracy theorist, well except maybe about whether man has actually walked on the moon, but that is a conversation for another time.

With the saboteur, let me go a little deeper.

The saboteur may also ask, "what will we do if this doesn't work?" This is technically still passive-aggressive, but a bit less passive and a bit more aggressive. Again, it plants the seeds of doubt, but perhaps a bit more direct. This question can put people in the mindset that there is a chance that we may go back to the old way... before we have even accepted the new method. Do not let this question go unchecked... ever.

This question can also place change leaders on the defensive, finding themselves explaining or even developing a contingency plan that they may not even need. Clever, right?

Let me keep going.
The saboteur may also ask this question:
"How did we come up with this as the change needed?" This question is even more treacherous. It questions the decision-making behind the change. It also creates a potential call to action to walk through the methodology of the change and creates potential rabbit holes- do not go there. If you lead a group that needs to work through the change, their only role is to work through the change. There are critical stages of involvement, and I believe necessary to get the ultimate level of buy-in. All that said, at the point of the rollout is not that time.

These are just some of the relatively simple and basic questions that the saboteur will ask. So basic and simple that you may not detect the malice inside.

I know some of you may think I am a bit too paranoid. Let me pull up to 50,000 feet and say this- no one really likes change. We tolerate it, accept it, and adjust to it, but we are not really asking for it. Not really.

A little more about the saboteur. The saboteur often fits the profile of the experienced, tenured person who is doing a good job, not to the level of being promoted, but well-placed for sure. Because of their profile in the organization, they may be highly respected by others. To that point, others around the table may not suspect them of sabotage at all.

The saboteur simply starts the fire and walks out of the house, leaving everyone else scrambling to find the fire extinguishers.

Depending on the level of deception by the saboteur, it may be the equivalent to them walking out of the house with the fire extinguishers in tow.

The Dissenter

You have heard the phrase- silence is consent. This is a very misleading statement that, in my opinion, does not get questioned often enough. Not only is silence <u>not</u> consent, but there are situations in which silence is dissent.

When we are excited about something, we are more likely to

declare it verbally or otherwise. Think about when you have learned that you are having your first child or have received a promotion at work or achieved a perfect score on a test.

With this level of excitement, you cannot wait to find someone to tell or to share it with.

Conversely, when you do not believe in something, and it causes you to have an adverse reaction, you are more likely to keep it to yourself.

Back to silence is more dissent. Just because a person does not openly display disagreement does not mean he/she is accepting what is being presented.
Here is an example:

You are sitting with a group of people talking about politics. Not sure why you would do that but let us go there. You discover ten minutes in the discussion that everyone around the table feels deeply passionate about one political party, and you are the only one that is passionate about the other party.

It can be an awkward situation. In this scenario, you may decide that you are outnumbered, and it is not worth the debate, so you stay silent. In this example, silence is not saying that you agree with the others at the table... at all. Furthermore, you violently disagree inside. That is dissent.

This same situation can play out when change is introduced. The dissenters are people around the table that violently disagree with the change... inside. Seeing everyone else around the table supporting the change may serve to make the holdout even more withdrawn and silent.

Dissenters are not always silent, though, but they are careful when they speak, where they speak, and who they speak to.

Here is another way of looking at the dissenter. The dissenter is the person who is likely to complain about the company that they work for, but never look to find a new job. You may say, well, if they are complaining, how can they also be a quiet voice. The way I answer that is this: They make sure that they are not complaining to anyone that can do anything about it. So, in this scenario, their boss would never hear about their disdain for the change from them and may never even hear it from anyone else about them.

Much like the saboteur, the dissenter does not want to be noticed, and they usually are not. Meanwhile, behind the scenes, they are quietly killing your change momentum and probably bringing down a lot of their co-workers.

The dissenter is not the biggest problem, but they are still a problem. You cannot underestimate their impact simply because of this: they are not complaining to their boss, which means they are bitching and moaning to others who were good with the change, but after having this dissenter in their ear, the supporters may also begin to rethink how they feel about the change.

So, do not underestimate the dissenter. Their ability to spread poison can be far-reaching.

One last point to contrast the dissenter to the saboteur. The saboteur is so stealth that they do not let anyone know what they are doing. At least the dissenter will share, giving a least a possibility of being discovered.

The Silent Assassin

The silent assassin is truly a quiet voice. They are not the saboteur, so they will not ask questions that could expose their resistance to the change. The silent assassin is also not the dissenter, who may share their displeasure with others that cannot do anything about the change, but still put themselves at risk of being exposed by doing so. Not the silent assassin. However, the silent assassins are not change agents either- they just do not verbally participate in the process... at all.

Silent assassins are generally quiet and introverted by nature, so whether there is change or not, you are not likely to hear from them.

Silent assassins have the potential to be as dangerous as the saboteur or the dissenter simply because you do not know where you stand with them. Because of their quiet demeanor, more often than not, we assume that they will be agreeable to the change. That can be a dangerous assumption.

One specific watch out. If you are a strong-willed leader that is accustomed to being dominant in conversation, you can miss one of the most important steps with this cohort- ask questions.

The silent assassin will be more than happy for a dominant leader to keep on talking- it means that they do not have to answer any questions. Additionally, you have to be careful because the silent assassin is skilled at listening to you talk and asking you questions to prevent the need for them to talk. Clever.

Of course, the silent assassin does not only exist in the workplace. Many of you unknowingly have silent assassins that you consider to be a part of your close circle. If you feel negative energy, consider who is in your close personal circle, and identify the outlier. If you are not sure, follow your intuition- it is usually correct.

Finally, the silent assassin understands tact and decorum and procedure. This serves to take you off their trail- that is what they want. You are so enamored with their kindness and generosity that you cannot possibly notice the fangs extending from their teeth.

Listen, I know it sounds like paranoia to think about these three groups and their intentions. If you have had a different experience than what I am describing, it does not mean that the saboteurs, the dissenters, and the silent assassins are not there; it could just be that you did not notice them.

Well, I did say that there is a positive element to all this- there is. When people are silent through the change process, they can also benefit you, so it is essential to have balance when assessing this.

On the positive side of the quiet voices, I believe that there are also three groups- contributors, digesters, and dog whistlers.

The Contributor

The contributor is the person who spends extraordinarily little time talking. So much so that you are not even sure that they are tracking with the change. The contributor leaves you wondering not only if they agree with the change, but whether they are even getting it.

The great news is that if you ask a contributor a question, you will likely get great insight. However, you have to ask.

I attended a board meeting many years ago, and one member of the board at the time was a former Senator and former NBA player- I will call him Bill. As I sat through the board meeting, Bill seemed to be the most disinterested. Not in a disrespectful way, but definitely not riveted with the conversation.

I do not believe that he fell asleep at any point during the meeting, but that might have been less distracting than his fidgeting, constant movement, and constant looking out into space.

I do recall a discussion about a strategic initiative that the company wanted to introduce. After much debate, Bill was called on for his input, not in a teacher-calling-out-the-nodding-student way. Instead, it was due to the high level of respect that the room had for Bill. Many that had been on the board also knew that Bill would not be very vocal. And then Bill was asked a question about the strategic initiative. His response was the most compelling train of thought of anything that was discussed that day. He went from appearing not to be paying attention to showing up as the smartest person in the room. Well, he probably was since he was a Rhodes Scholar!

The contributor is very measured. They are not interested in being the center of attention or even showing up as the smartest person in the room, but they, in fact, may be the smartest person in the room.

So, the key to bringing out the best in the contributor merely is getting them to talk. It is usually not what they want to do, but under the right circumstances, they will share, and you will likely be glad that they did.

The Digester

This is the let-me-think-about-it-and-get-back-to-you person. This person can drive you nuts. You just want their opinion, and they will not give it to you.

The digester is cautious by nature- put them in an environment of change, and they will likely withdraw even more. It is never an issue of whether they understand the change or agree with the change.

The digester is the person that you want to speak up about change, but they will not- they must go through their process of processing.

It does not matter because the digester will not tip their hand to you on what they are thinking, even though they may agree with the change. Where the digester is valuable to you is that you can be confident that when they do come back to you after their time to think about the change, the digester will present questions or viewpoints that will likely impress you.

There is a risk with the digester, though. Showing frustration for their lack of communication and pushing the digester too hard to share could tip them over to changing their view about the change and no longer support it. So, be careful.

When it comes to change, the digester will not share their view of the change with others- while that is not necessarily positive, it is as least not negative. They will not engage in office gossip, but they will not necessarily stop it either. They will simply take inventory of everything they see and hear, and after careful analysis, they will provide insight. It will be on their schedule, though.

The Dog Whistler

Dog whistle is nomenclature related to politics, art, sciences, etc.; however, it could apply to any subject.

Figuratively, a 'dog whistle' is a coded message communicated through words or phrases commonly only understood by a particular group of people.

The dog whistler, when it comes to the change process, is someone who is trying to help you- they just do not want to do it directly.

The dog whistler has likely been exposed to information that would help you identify the saboteurs, dissenters, and silent assassins and better utilize the contributors and digesters.

However, somewhere in their professional or personal life, the dog whistler has had an experience that backfired. They spoke up, and it was used against them. They vow that will never happen to them again, so as much as their instincts tell them that they should speak up and be helpful, they will only do so under circumstances that ensure their anonymity.

The dog whistler will literally leave you breadcrumbs, letters, notes, but never anything directly.

If you can ever identify this person, you are paying attention as a leader. A wink and a nod are all you will need from that point on but be careful because overexposing or overutilizing information from the dog whistler can put their identity at risk. You do not want to seem too smart in utilizing the context the dog whistler shares to address the gaps in the change process you are implementing.

Last thing here, let me share a couple of stories about quiet voices. Honestly, they do not have a lot to do with the change process itself, but they were very impactful and taught me a lesson about being more aware.

I did an executive market visit in Houston many years ago. There were four high-level leaders on this visit. I recall us all going behind the line, to the back of the restaurant, to meet the employees. The second employee that I shook hands with was not nervous about our visit. He was not overly excited either... he appeared mentally to be somewhere else. His eyes said, leave me alone, and I need help, all at the same time. It was a confusing look that I did not recall seeing before or even seeing since then. After meeting thousands of employees over the years, it was odd to see something new.

If you asked the employee later who came to visit the store, he would not be able to pick us out of a lineup. The blank stare on his face was troublesome, but I did not know what to do with it. So, I did nothing.

On that day, this employee was a quiet voice, but so was I. I could have and should have been more curious. I vowed not to ever do that again.

A few months later, I had a market visit to Orange County in California. As a part of the tour, we were visiting a store where the store manager was presented with the manager of the year award for that region. That region was over 600 stores, so this was a pretty big deal.

I could see the anticipation on the faces of the regional

vice-president, the regional director, and the district manager. When the time arrived, we all showed up in the store with balloons and cake to celebrate. The store manager was awarded a plaque by the regional vice-president, and he was clearly proud of his team and their accomplishments. Many of his employees came into the store that day to celebrate with him- a sign of a true servant leader. It appeared to be one of the happiest days of his life... it appeared.

A few weeks later, I received a call from the regional vice-president, informing me that this same store manager had committed suicide. I was numb.

Of course, numb because a life was lost. Even more numb because this life was lost. How could that be? He was just beaming with joy and pride only weeks earlier. Everyone was shocked. The store manager's roommate was another store manager in the area, and he was shocked. No one saw it coming, no one.

The quiet voices.

No one knew the changes that were happening in the life of this store manager. He was a quiet voice in a very loud space. He operated a store where everyone knew everyone, where his employees came in to hang out on their off day. He was everything to them, and they were everything to him. And yet... this is how powerful quiet voices are.

This store manager clearly had changes occurring in his life that no one knew about and, apparently, he went to great lengths to ensure that no one knew.

When change is happening, you need the quiet voices- you need to identify them, seek them out, and listen to them.

What I know is that change evokes emotion in all of us, and sometimes it can create powerful emotion.

No matter how long I lead, I will always remember that store manager and his successes and, unfortunately, the tragedy that came with his story.

Whether the change is personal or professional, it is important to recognize it and have a process to manage through it. I believe that it is time to start thinking about the change process in a different way. Perhaps, it is time to take change in a new direction.

CHAPTER 6:

The Change Hook

There are many published philosophies regarding change management- I am going to introduce one more that I am attaching to the change approach. Specifically, to help you break through the Hostility Of Change.

It is a principle that I developed called:

"The Change Hook."

The Change Hook

The Change Hook states that when change is introduced, no one stays in the same place emotionally- either you are for the change or against the change. It is a belief that no one is indifferent to change.

The Change Hook also states that people that are champions of the change- change agents- immediately move towards the new change.

However, those opposed to change, change-averse, immediately move in the opposite direction at first. Even when those who are change-averse become aligned, they have a much longer journey back to the point of accepting real, sustainable change.

I have thought about how to articulate this concept many times over the years. As I have been exposed to organizational changes, I have learned about many different versions of change models. Contrasting The Change Hook to other change models was the breakthrough that helped me determine how to share this.

Many change models go through the stages of shock, denial, frustration, depression, experiment, decision, and integration. Other model examples include phases such as anger, despair, acceptance, exploration, and resolution. Many of these change models are strikingly similar in philosophy and application.

Strikingly similar in that most of them assume a continuum – the belief that people start in one place and progress through phases until they arrive at embracing the new change. I am not sure that human behavior is that predictable because of the emotion, the hostility that comes along with change.

I recognize that some may believe that people do not move either way when change is introduced. That could be true... but not likely. Here is why:

Real change evokes such emotion that it is difficult for us as human beings to not react to it, to not move in one direction or the other. The more directly the change affects us, the greater the potential of emotion and the greater the potential of movement in either direction- towards acceptance of the change or resistance to the change.

Perhaps when people do not move either way when change is introduced, it is not change being introduced, just improvement. Not to minimize improvement, but "improvement is not the same as change." We will cover that in a later chapter.

As you follow my writings, you will find that things are meant to be linked together. For example, part of what creates this change-averse mentality when change is introduced is the deep-seated bias discussed earlier in the book. When change is presented that is inconsistent with your personal biases, the first reaction is to reject the change- you are change-averse. Not only do you not accept the change, but you also move away from the change. The visual of that is a long journey to get to acceptance, if and when you accept it.

The best way to describe The Change Hook is to share real-life situations involving change- one that I experienced and one that I observed.

I recall a few years ago when I was still working at Starbucks, and we first entertained the notion of changing our logo.

You must understand the importance of the logo at Starbucks. I am sure that there is a story behind most company logos created, but many have not made an emotional connection between the brand and the logo in the way that Starbucks has.

At Starbucks, the logo is tied to so much storytelling about the brand- the siren story in the center of the logo and how Starbucks evolved from the early days of selling coffee, tea, and spices, to where they have evolved to today.

In 1971, when the only Starbucks store was in Pike Place Market in Seattle, Starbucks' founders desired to have a symbol that encompassed both the maritime history of coffee and Seattle's strong seaport roots.

After going through tons of materials, the answer revealed itself- the Siren. The 16th-century Norse woodcut of a twin-tailed mermaid had both a mystery about her mixed with a nautical theme, and now, for almost fifty years, the Siren has been at the heart of the Starbucks logo.

A part of the logo journey that many may not be aware of is that, in the beginning, the Siren was topless, and even though Starbucks received many complaints from customers, they chose to keep the logo the way it was. It is difficult to believe that a brand could face that type of scrutiny today and not give in to the pressure to change. Of course, it was 1971, Starbucks was a tiny company at the time, and there was no social media.

Starbucks CEO Howard Schultz, when asked about the logo years later, explained that part of the approach way back when was that the mermaid "was supposed to be as seductive as the coffee itself." You could get away with that in the 'good old days.'

As the company started to grow, Starbucks began utilizing delivery trucks, which became problematic since the topless Siren was prominently displayed on the trucks. Hence, the growth of Starbucks created the need for the first logo change.

So, when Howard Schultz first became the CEO in 1986, the logo was changed. The Siren's hair was restyled, the company name was shortened to Starbucks Coffee, and the text ring around the Siren also changed, losing the words tea and spices. It would be a precursor to what was to come with the later logo change, but again- this was way back in 1986, small company and no social media.

Oh, and the primary logo color changed from brown to green.

Just six years later, in 1992, Starbucks was a publicly-traded stock for the first time. Around that time, another slight logo change occurred. The Siren's face became the point of emphasis, with lines changing ever so slightly and a closer in view of the Siren, giving the logo a more corporate feel.

With both these logo changes, Starbucks was still relatively unknown in many communities in the United States. However, over the next nineteen years, the growth of Starbucks took off. The logo was put on every cup, and people proudly carried their Starbucks cup worldwide as a status symbol. The Starbucks logo even became part of pop culture as it was prominently displayed in movies. In fact, in the 1990s and 2000s, it was almost expected to see a Starbucks cup placement in any significant movie. Starbucks, I mean Farbucks, even showed up in Shrek!

Fast forward to 2011 and, as one of the most recognized brands in the world, Starbucks was about to embark upon yet another logo change.

This change would involve removing the outer ring making the Siren the sole focus of the logo design. We decided to remove the outer ring to not be defined by coffee only in future generations. We had aspirations to take the brand in broader platforms. The strategy of it made perfect sense then, which happened to be when the company turned forty years old.

I could have chosen the book title because of this specific story alone. Just a few hours after introducing the new logo, there was a hostile public response.

The Change Hook was evoked.

There was a significant backlash against the logo change building on social media and the Starbucks website. Many customers did not like the change and made it known. Based on the feedback from so many customers, the overall sentiment was that the change seemed random and unnecessary. Of course, those who were already not fans of the brand took the liberty to pile on.

At that time, anything that Starbucks did got the attention of the media, fair or not; there was always scrutiny, people looking for a reason to bash the brand. However, this was not that- this was all self-imposed. With this change, we created the fodder for late-night television hosts and bloggers and hand-delivered it to them.

The customer response was actually the easy part- then there was the employee response. If you have never worked for Starbucks, you may still not understand why this is such a big deal.

The outer ring of the logo was eliminated. It effectively meant that we were dropping the name Starbucks Coffee from the logo. To many of our partners (what we called our employees), the mere conversation of it was laughable at first. I mean, we were a coffee company through and through. What many quickly learned was that this was not laughable at all. In fact, it invoked anger and tears.

I have thought about this many times attempting to understand why the partner response was so negative. This is where I come out: It was a combination of factors- even though Starbucks was evolving with the advent of music, books, and movie offerings, it was still a total surprise to the field, it was an ultimatum, and it evoked emotion. It also threatened another emotional part of the business- culture. Culture at Starbucks is everything- much more so than anywhere else that I have worked. Culture is a topic for another book.

The emotional response amongst partners was swift, and many moved immediately to the change-averse side of The Change Hook. It was mutiny. I know it sounds melodramatic, but there was a real, visceral reaction inside the organization, especially in the stores, where coffee was just as sacred as it was in Seattle, maybe even more sacred.

Back to an earlier point in the book:

For some, change is an ultimatum.

When you thrust change upon someone, by surprise, without consent, without alignment, and without agreement, it is basically an ultimatum... and you should, at the very least, anticipate a hostile response.

There is more to this story, though. Sometimes change can be amplified by other environmental factors. Such was the case with this logo change at Starbucks being impacted by my other story.

So, onto the second experience...

The drama that was playing out impacting this logo change at Starbucks was that it was occurring immediately after the number one clothing chain, GAP, had just gone through a logo change that can only be described as what we would call today- an epic fail.

In early October 2010, in what appeared to come out of nowhere, the GAP changed its logo and surprised everyone. As I often say- '99% of all surprises in business are negative'... and so was this one.

The logo change at the GAP was a new clean font, with a small blue square overlapping the "P." It was goodbye to the twenty-year-old solid blue square and the capital letters and hello to Helvetica and a little blue patch.

It was described as more contemporary and current. It was meant to honor the heritage through the blue box while still taking it forward.

It was... a hot mess.

There was a significantly more hostile reaction to the GAP logo change than the Starbucks logo change. Incidentally, this logo change for the GAP was also occurring around the fortieth anniversary of the brand.

In addition to the hostile reaction to the look of the logo itself, the GAP had made no effort to change their product line, revamp their stores, and, most importantly, signal to their customers that a change was coming. They simply changed the logo.

It just did not make any sense, and the resulting backlash was instant... hostile.

The Change Hook was evoked... again.

Some of the adjectives used by GAP customers to describe the new logo were less than flattering, and mostly, they were not fit for print. The addition of the blue square seemed to be hated on a united front by customers - many felt that it just looked cheap and tacky.

As a result, only days later, the fashion leader folded and reverted to the solid blue box's original logo and "GAP" written in a capitalized serif font. The logo change and change back happened so fast that many people did not even notice it. However, those that did notice it made their feelings well known.

There is something to the challenge that large corporations have of divulging too much information and risk exposing an impending change in a manner that takes away the surprise of it, especially publicly-traded companies. However, not socializing an idea broadly enough can leave you with the element of surprise. When that change also comes as a surprise inside of the organization, it is well, even more surprising.

As this story has been written repeatedly, most of the blame has consistently pointed at one executive. I will not name names here. My view is that it was an epic collapse by many even to allow this idea to get past all levels of internal vetting and get to the finish line.

In the end, if the GAP, a very recognizable American brand, missed the mark this badly with a logo change, the Starbucks change of removing the brand name and the word coffee from the logo seemed to be a really, really bad idea at the time.

So, back to the Starbucks logo change. The change happened, and we all lived- partners and customers. In the end, it was fine. However, when we are talking about real, sustainable change, that is not good enough. Bringing people along on the journey is a component of successful change implementation.

The damage done by the emotional hostility created does not merely go away overnight... and sometimes not at all. Even when people are over the material change that occurred, they are often left remembering the emotion of the change. You had better hope that it is good emotion.

There are times when the principal leaders involved in developing and implementing the change have been working on it for so long behind the scenes that they have long since worked through the emotional part of the change. By the time they bring the change to market, their awareness of the emotion that may come with the change is long gone. That is not an indictment of leaders; that is more of a human element, but one that best-in-class leaders will recognize, remember, and bring forward that emotion for when the big reveal occurs.

Perhaps it is like a father finding out that his daughter just landed a promotion. There is a rush of emotion. The father says, do not tell your mother until she returns from her business trip to tell her face-to-face. No matter how excited the father is, days later, when the daughter tells her mother the news in the presence of the father, it is not likely that he can replicate the emotion that he had when he heard it the first time.

So, back to The Change Hook.

There are several takeaways here:

The negative consequences of change are always amplified far more than the benefits of the change.

This is a tenet of change. It is often easier, conveniently easier, to gravitate towards the negative aspect of change- why it will not work.

It is difficult to put a percentage on the number of people that are change agents versus being change-averse. I have had a leader share that he believes that it is 15% change agents and 85% change-averse. If I had to assign a percent, I would agree with his assessment. If true, it is another data point that amplifies how difficult change really is.

Second, change has nothing to do with logical, rational, well-thought-out strategies. All that most of your teams will hear is that there is change, and frankly, that means things are not the same. Of course, things could get better, but more than likely, they gravitate to things could get worse.

In the end, all that your team will be thinking about are any one of those dreaded eight-word phrases:

> "This is the way it's always been done."
> "Things are fine the way that they are."
> "If it is not broke, don't fix it."
> "We tried that before, and it didn't work."

By the way, to further amplify the misstep by the GAP, they have changed their logo again since the 2010 debacle. In 2016, the GAP introduced a new logo: their current logo, with little to no fanfare... and most importantly, no hostility.

Hmmm, interesting how the lack of hostility and acceptance of change can work together. As I recall, there was not much lead-in to this second logo change by the GAP, perhaps because it looks a whole lot like the original logo. Yes, doing something that generally makes sense can be widely accepted, even without prior notice... especially when it is deemed sensible to the point that it invokes the smallest emotional response possible. Okay.

The story of both logo changes is a position of defense. The change was introduced, and in both instances, the change had to be defended. The approach with either brand does not represent the offensive position necessary to implement real, sustainable change.

As a leader, your role is about more than just getting agreement or alignment on the change- you must make a case for change.

Making a case for change means getting people to the place emotionally where they believe there is no option other than to accept the change. Creating a belief so strong that they wonder why this change has not already occurred.

Making a case for change involves investing time with your people to ensure that there are no misunderstandings; there is a clear "what's in it for them," a straightforward process and timeline to follow, and time dedicated to questions to get people comfortable with the change.

...and that is just table stakes.

To go further, you may have to compartmentalize how you think about presenting the change based on different personalities and leadership styles. For example, some will be sold on the change because of the financial implications. A subset of the group will only be moved to accept the change because of the productivity aspect- the work environment becomes better. Some will only buy-in to the change because it is different- it breaks up the monotony of the job. Others will adapt to change simply because they are supportive of the leader and trust their direction.

Beyond all that, the case for change is truly made when you provide inspiration. When you get people genuinely excited about the change, you make it memorable; you make it easy to remember and recite, you make it stick.

With the right inspiration, you can influence The Change Hook by making more people change agents, and even by influencing faster adoption in those who were initially change-averse.

I know. You probably think that this is a high bar. No doubt it is. For real, sustainable change to occur, it is.

So how do you embed real, sustainable change?
Well, a key element is understanding the difference between improvement and change.

CHAPTER 7:

Improvement Is Not The Same As Change

One aspect of breaking through the hostility of change is this principle:

Improvement is not the same as change.

So often, we confuse improvement for change. Do not get me wrong; recognizing improvement is very important. In some cases, it is a critical step to eventually get to change, eventually being the keyword here.

Real, sustainable change is not methodical. Real, sustainable change skips incrementality.

In fact, the change curve models that I referenced earlier are arguably a journey through improvement- all great... but not real, sustainable change. That is not to knock the effectiveness of any of them.

I know- I have been referencing "real, sustainable change" chapter after chapter, so what am I talking about here?

Real, sustainable change is swift, sudden, noticeable, different, and of course, permanent.   For example:

Real, sustainable change is smoking three packs of cigarettes a day for twenty years, and tomorrow, deciding to stop smoking and never smoke again.

Real, sustainable change is losing a hundred pounds in six months from exercising and eating healthier... and keeping the weight off. A hundred pounds is an arbitrary number- of course, it needs to be weight loss relative to the starting weight that is significant enough to be life-changing weight loss.

In this example of weight loss, if you have lost pounds over a few months and people you have not seen during that time see you again, and do not comment about your weight loss, then that is improvement, not change. Again, do not be disappointed as improvement is important; it is just not dramatic enough to be considered real change.

Improvement is gradual. So just more of the same thing improving at the pace of the environment around you is not materially different- acceptable and often rewarded, but not different. On the other hand, change evokes something new, something different, a complete departure from what you are comfortable with, and sometimes a break from what you already know.

Real change should require a conscious effort- there is no previously learned pattern; therefore, it takes thought and focus and even extensive practice.

Without a conscious effort, the adaptability needed is minimal, and therefore, it is not real change.

Try untying your shoes and retying them in the opposite direction or folding your arms and then unfolding them and folding them the opposite way. What you are likely to find with both these activities is that it takes a conscious effort to do either activity differently. This is not improvement- this is change. It is something different, immediate, and requires a focused, conscious effort to make it happen... and this is on something remarkably simple.

Conversely, untying your shoes and then retying them in the same manner but doing it faster is improvement. Does that make sense?

You got better at the process, but it is not really different, and it did not really require a conscious effort.

All that said, this chapter is not about minimizing the importance of improvement. But, to get to change, we need to better understand what improvement is and is not.

Improvement is the process of getting better. The distinction here is that better can be over any period; therein lies the trap. It is one of the most prominent differences between improvement and change. At times, it is tricky to be able to discern what is improvement versus what is change.

Real, sustainable change is tied more to timing and timing of the results, not process.

In business, improvement should be celebrated. However:

Do not settle for improvement when you are expecting change. More importantly, do not settle for improvement when you need change.

To that end, there are situations in which improvement can be interpreted as unfavorable. Case in point, an improvement over negative performance could still be substandard performance. It may be improvement, but it does not mean that you should be satisfied with it or reward it.

Back to my point about the change models that exist today-there are times when a change process is so process-oriented that it takes too long, and ultimately it is interpreted as just improvement.

It was late 2014, and the tattoo policy at Starbucks was changing to allow employees to have visible tattoos. Until that time, at Starbucks, we were faced with the challenge that all retailers have been faced with- to allow visible tattoos or not allow visible tattoos.

The collective morality and ethical beliefs of the consumer have long been at the center of the conversation across executive boardrooms of many companies, large and small, who have had to wrestle with the issue over the past decade of allowing visible tattoos.

The fear of the consumer rejecting the establishment because of the allowance of visible tattoos by an organization still permeates through many executive boardrooms. Really? Let us examine the ground truth behind this:

Never mind that now, according to Dalia Research on medium. com, almost 50% of all American adults have a tattoo and a large majority, over 75% of them, have more than one tattoo. However, according to historyoftattoos.com, more than 70% of Americans with tattoos keep them hidden.

Perhaps there is still a taboo associated with tattoos... from the 50% that do not have one.

As I have worked to get to the ground truth over the past few years from conversations with many executive leaders, it became clear that the barrier was not the customer. It was the executives themselves. Now, none of them said that to me directly. However, as they described their belief system, it was the evidence that I needed to conclude that the consumer had nothing to do with the policies that existed in their organizations.

The feedback from these executives did yield this: these are executives who collectively believe that employees should not have piercings, should have to wear a uniform, and should have 100% open availability. Happy recruiting because you will be hard-pressed to find enough potential front line employees that meet your unrealistic, lofty standards.

The "when I was growing up," monologue came up from executive leaders on more than one occasion. It was disappointing, but it reflected the reality of the situation, the barrier.

After all, Best Buy and many other mainstream companies had been amongst the early adopters of allowing employees with visible tattoos with little concern shared from their customers. Perhaps, Best Buy was more focused on the "showrooming" behavior that caused their business to move online more rapidly than most retailers than to deal with a pesky tattoo policy.

It all came full circle for me in early 2015 at Starbucks when I held an open forum attended by approximately 100 employees. This was soon after we announced the change to our policy, allowing visible tattoos.

I was confident that the topic of tattoos would come up during this open forum and, given our recent announcement, I was feeling optimistic. I welcomed any potential questions on this topic.

About thirty minutes into the session, an employee raised his hand and asked for clarification about the tattoo policy. His question was not directed towards any part of the new policy or to even ask for the policy to be even more relaxed. By the way, there were still some limitations like no neck or face tattoos. Instead, he looked at me with a look of disappointment and said, "what took us so long to change the policy?"

I must admit that I did not see that question coming.

Of course, I did not take the look of disappointment personally, but perhaps I should have. I mean, I was a big supporter to allow visible tattoos from the very beginning. In the end, though, I was part of the senior operations team, and, fair or not, I was lumped in with the group that had demonstrated a level of resistance to allow visible tattoos for some time.

Visible tattoos were never a big deal to me, especially since most other retailers had already demonstrated a progressive approach. Most importantly, the employee workforce has long since moved on from the issue and considered tattoos to be table stakes inside a dress code policy. This only stood to challenge us more as we were left in a relatively small minority amongst significant retailers who were not allowing visible tattoos.

Let me back up and talk about how we got here.

In 2013, one of our proudest moments at Starbucks was when we announced that we would hire 10,000 veterans and their spouses over the following five years. Huge credit to Starbucks after I left the company as they did achieve that goal far sooner than planned and had hired more than double that amount by 2018. However, as we began to hire veterans and their spouses in 2014, we were exposed to a different challenge.

What challenge? Almost every research statistic points to members of the military collectively having more tattoos than their civilian counterparts.

By hiring so many military members, it forced our hand at re-examining our policy on visible tattoos. It would be unfair to conclude that this is the only reason that we relented on our policy. There was enough of a societal groundswell already from tens of thousands of Starbucks employees wanting us to allow visible tattoos.

However, we had no choice but to acknowledge that it may seem disingenuous to turn away current and former soldiers and even their spouses due to visible tattoos after making such a public announcement. Moreover, as we interviewed many of them and found them to be the most qualified candidates, it made even less sense to allow visible tattoos to be a barrier.

In the end, an employee asking the question, 'what took us so long to change the policy' is more of an indictment of us moving too slow and not keeping pace with the times. It is like telling someone to duck after an airborne item has already struck them. Our timing was simply not that effective.

In the end, we improved, but we did not make real change- that was reserved for the early movers, the risk-takers. That is how many employees collectively viewed it, and we had to own that. For sure, a case study in decision-making in the generation in which we currently live.

Now let me share a much broader story that gets at initiating real, sustainable change instead of improvement:

In early 2008, I was working for Starbucks as a regional vice-president. Life was good, and business was good. By early 2009, life was still good, business not so much.

At Starbucks, we were trying to figure out the shifting business dynamics just like everyone else. We needed to turn the business around and turn it around fast.

To that point, Howard Schultz had returned as CEO in February of 2008, just before the economic collapse. We struggled through 2008 like everyone else, and then I received a call from our president of U.S. retail in early 2009. He called to share that Howard was in Dallas visiting with one of our board members and wanted to visit stores with me the next morning.

Yes, that was the "advanced" notice that I received.
At that point in my career, though, I had already learned to have a market visit presentation ready for any major visits or any unexpected visits. Well, this was major and unexpected.

Until this time at Starbucks, I had shaken hands with Howard a couple of times but had never had a conversation with him... that was about to change.

I met Howard the next morning in the lobby of the Ritz-Carlton hotel in downtown Dallas. To my surprise, it was just Howard- no entourage. At that time, it was very uncommon to see Howard anywhere without a group of executives with him. Having been back in the CEO role for a little less than a year, Howard usually spent time out in market calibrating with those on his executive team.

For me, this was an opportunity- an opportunity to spend time with Howard in a way that I knew many long-tenured employees may not have ever had. So, I seized it.

Considering the business climate at the time, I was pleasantly surprised when Howard seemed happy and ready to take on the day.

As we began to discuss the day, Howard stated that he wanted to visit three stores and then have me take him to the hangar to fly back to Seattle.

I quickly answered back without hesitation - "I believe that it is important to always set context about what you are going to see in stores, so I would like to go over a business review before heading out."

And then there was the awkward silence- the 'are-you-telling-me-what-to-do' kind of awkward silence. It was not a long silence, I am sure, but it felt like minutes as I braced for Howard's response. On one hand, was I too bold? Had I gone too far? Had I misread his body language? It felt as though I had time to ask myself all sorts of questions and all the possible answers and scenarios while waiting on his response. I began to think that this could be the shortest market visit ever.

On the other hand, I thought, what is the worst that can happen?

Howard finally responded with, "sure."

So, we sat down in the lobby, just the two of us, and talked shop. I shared a bit about the region, the team, the results. Honestly, the region had a great story to share, so I wanted to make sure that it was heard. Not in a self-serving way but more about seizing the moment. It was one of my proudest moments- mainly being able to talk about our talent and how they were leading and developing.

The business review lasted about an hour. Howard did not ask many questions, but his head nodding gave me the confidence that I needed to continue to walk him through the review.

Then, it was time for store visits. As soon as we got into the car, Howard said, "today, there will be a crisis somewhere in the world." A big statement, a strong statement- one that demonstrated just how significant his role was as CEO.

We left for the stores. We visited three stores, and Howard was indeed a servant leader on those visits, sitting across the table from the store manager of each store with his focus exclusively on them. It was even more remarkable as I reflected on his statement of when we got into the car only a few minutes earlier. Being able to balance the broad and narrow aspect of the role- that was leadership.

We spent a couple of hours in the three stores in total. After that, I took Howard to the hangar, and he left for Seattle.

On these types of visits, you do not often get feedback in the moment and sometimes not at all. Nonetheless, I waited for feedback. And waited and waited. Two weeks had gone by and nothing. I began to think, that is it... I blew it.

Finally, after two and a half weeks, I got a call from the president of U.S. retail late one evening. He said, "Oh yeah, I wanted to let you know that I talked to Howard, and he said that his trip to Dallas with you was the best field business review that he has ever had." Well, that was certainly worth the wait! I understood the magnitude of those comments straight away. What I did not know was how that would change my future at Starbucks.

I received another call from the president of U.S. retail about a week later stating that Howard wants to take the next Starbucks board meeting out of Seattle and bring it to Dallas.

I was blown away. At that time, all board meetings were held in Seattle. Whether the choice to take it to Dallas was all about my visit, the fact that one of the board members lived there, or a combination of both, it did not matter.

I recall sharing the news with the team in Dallas, and I could see their excitement... and concern. This was a big deal.

This visit meant a lot of activity would be occurring leading up to the board meeting- this meant renovating stores, this meant prepping the leadership team on financials and roles, this meant initiating facilities work, and most of all, this meant having the right people in place for the stores that we picked to be a part of the market visits and those stores that were positioned close to the location of the board meeting to be prepared.

As this news was sinking in with the team, it was also sinking in with me.

Once I got word of the board meeting coming to Dallas, I had a conversation with my boss at the time to talk with the president of U.S. retail on my behalf. I had one request- if the board meeting was going to be in my market, I wanted to attend. I knew that the opportunity for exposure could not get any bigger than this or any more convenient than this. The response back to me within days was yes, you can attend.

A couple of weeks later, I called my boss again. I said, "can you talk to the president again and ask him, since I am already going to be at the board meeting, can I present something?" My boss took that message back on my behalf, and again, a couple of weeks later, the answer was yes.

I was fully aware that I was testing the limits, but hey, I was riding the wave of momentum, and I understood the opportunity with this platform to push key messaging up in the organization.

I must admit, I was consumed with this market opportunity- it is all I thought about for the weeks and months leading up to the board meeting.

I was going to prepare the presentation of all presentations. I was going to dazzle the board. I was going to control the room.

I... needed to figure out what I was going to say. I knew this- I needed to say something bold, something memorable.

The Starbucks Board at that time was an accomplished board- they had truly seen and heard just about everything. I mean, we even had a former NBA player, former Senator and Rhodes scholar, on the board!

So, the preparation began. I knew the state of the business, I knew the risk of us doing nothing, and I knew the risk of just improving. We needed change- real, sustainable change. And we needed to break through our hubris. Yes, as I referenced with Blockbuster earlier in the book, hubris was prevalent at Starbucks too. Not always intentional but ever-present. However, hubris almost always comes with being a leader in your industry, so it was not unique to Starbucks at that time.

Now that activities were in motion in preparation for the board meeting, I was scheduled for market visits the following week in Houston. As I was talking out loud about the upcoming board meeting with the two regional directors in Houston, one of them was sharing about how he was teaching business acumen amongst his team. Some remarkably simple, but effective tactics that seemed to be cutting through the barriers that had prevented store managers, and especially assistant managers, from growing key business and financial acumen skills.

The discussion that we were having sparked ideas about how not just to grow the top of the P&L with sales or the bottom of the P&L with profits, but also the middle of the P&L with expenses and costs. But there was more- a conversation about gross margin and distribution costs was key to all of this.

As I left Houston, I began to zero in on what is possible if we were delivering on all these financial components.

At the time, the region I led was the best performing region in the company from a sales perspective and, more importantly, from a profit perspective. Given the economy and many customers' decision to cut into their five-dollar-a-day Starbucks habit based on the economic recession, growing sales was not the winning proposition that it had always been. Let me take that a step further- not only were sales not increasing, they were declining and, for the first time in our company's history, we were faced with negative comparable sales in our stores.

I also knew that I could not afford to be so myopic to look at growing profits without giving people a roadmap to get there.

My region was operating at a 16% store level margin, while the U.S. overall was operating at around 11% store level margin. I knew that from examining P&Ls from across the country that our 16% had some advantages, like lower occupancy costs, but we were also winning on the controllable metrics. However, what I believed to be true was that, wherever the U.S. regions were performing on store-level margin, we could be better- I honestly believed that.

With gross margin, costs, and profits in my head, I devised a strategy. I believed that, when the recession ended, we would regain sales, and that would help us recover some level of profits just based on flow-thru. However, I identified that as improvement. I feared that, as the environment improved, we would improve, and it would feel good, and we would celebrate it, but with a full understanding that most of those results would not be a direct reflection of our operational expertise.

I would not accept that. I knew that 18%, 19%, even 20% total contribution (store level margin) would be in reach over the next two to three years- that is improvement. I believed that we could get to 25% total contribution- that is change. Candidly, if I had proposed a plan to get to 19% total contribution, I would have put the board to sleep.

I also knew that getting to 25% store level margin, or total contribution, would not be possible without getting to 50% on costs- what we called controllable contribution, and I knew that getting to 50% controllable contribution would not be possible without getting to 75% gross margin.

What I learned is that when you are looking to implement change across a broad group- in this case, 620 stores, and more than 10,000 employees, a mantra becomes a crucial part of telling the story and making the change stick.

And so, the "75-50-25" mantra was born. This mantra became the rallying cry within the team, but more importantly, within the stores. I also learned that the simplicity of the message and the nice round numbers that came with it was easily remembered, easily recitable, and easy to share.

I began to message it in emails, voicemails, reporting, and mostly through recognition. Of course, I reinforced it on store visits. Before long, it was the thing. It was what I was known for as a regional vice-president, and it was what I wanted to be known for... and that becomes a legacy.

Legacy- that is a critical leadership word. I will not digress here to discuss legacy, but I will come back to it later in the book.

Over the next few months, the region saw an acceleration in all three areas- gross margin, controllable contribution, and total contribution. The recognition was flowing, and so was the healthy competition. It was just the momentum that I needed to tell the story at the upcoming board meeting.

The day had finally arrived for the board meeting- September 16, 2009.

I must admit, as I walked into the board meeting and looked around the room, it was a bit intimidating.

However, what I had to take inventory of was the fact that I knew more about the Starbucks operation than anyone in the room. I knew that, and I believed that. More importantly, I presented like that.

No doubt, a board of directors may have the most prevalent deep-seated views of anyone of how the business should operate, and I believed that to be true of the Starbucks Board. After all, you assemble a board based on their expertise.

I had thirty minutes to tell the story... and I did. I weaved a message about the region, its people, the results, the stores, what they would see in stores, and yes, 75-50-25. I said that we would deliver it over the next two years and a quarter- particularly the 25% store level margin.

It was a bold move. It did not seem realistic, but it seemed necessary. I was maniacal about 75-50-25. During the run-up to the board meeting, I was so focused on 75-50-25 that I saw no possible way to fail. My euphoria for it had outweighed my common sense and, I could have been presenting the plan to the Queen of England at the time, and I would have been bold enough to still commit to it. That is what real change looked like to me.

This was the moment that I broke through at Starbucks. This was real change, and one component of real, sustainable change is that there has to be a departure from what is normal, what is expected, and mostly what is possible.

I had lost my mind. Stepping out to do something deemed to be impossible was liberating. Of course, I left the board room that day with a bit of uh-oh, what did I just do? Then my incredible team quickly moved to do it and delivered on it.

Improvement would have looked and sounded like all other presentations. Improvement would have been happy to have incremental progress. Improvement would have been happy to stay number one in profit and many other key performance metrics. Improvement would have been happy to celebrate success. Improvement would not have been change.

Of course, the story has a positive ending. I would not be telling this story if we had not reached the goal of 75-50-25. We achieved a 19% store level margin by the end of 2009, a 22.8% store level margin by the end of 2010, and a 25.7% store level margin by the end of 2011. By that time, not only was the region exceeding 75% on gross margin, 50% on controllable contribution, and 25% on total contribution, we had the highest percentage of total stores reaching each of those targets.

Fast forward to the spring of 2018. I had left Starbucks and gone to work for Jamba Juice as the chief operating officer. I was in my Jamba office in Frisco, Texas, and received a call from a former colleague who said that they were attending a meeting in Seattle in which the same president of U.S. retail was talking to a room of leaders. Part of this speech involved the retelling of the 75-50-25 story. The fact that this story was still being told almost nine years later made me feel good about what the team had accomplished and what it did to change the trajectory of results at Starbucks across the U.S. business.

Telling a team that you are number one but that is not good enough is threading the needle for sure, but it is also leadership that demonstrates that you are driving for real, sustainable change.

Real, sustainable change is going after what is possible, not what is best-in-class.

After all, beyond your best is better. With that, when you are presented with change, you might as well align your choices to be the best ones possible.

CHAPTER 8:

Change Is A Choice

On the most basic level, change is a choice. No matter how persuasive you may be at influencing change, ultimately, others have the option, the choice, of accepting the change or not.

On the receiving end of change, you may not like the choices you have, but you always have options, and therefore, change can always be accepted or rejected.

The debate about whether your choices are good or bad is a different discussion. Even when all of your options are bad, you are still faced with making a choice. Choices that come as a result of a life-or-death situation may not be sustainable. When the conditions change or said differently- get better, you are likely to abandon the perceived forced choice that you had to make previously.

I have always believed that choice is the most significant expression of free will- our ability to shape our life almost minute to minute with our available options.

To effectively manage an organizational change, it is critical to understand and accept that people have choices. Because people are free to choose from a broad range of options, a project will only succeed if the choices you need them to make turn out to be the choices that are agreeable to them.

Many organizations operate from a top-down approach. The risk is that people may comply with what they are ordered to do, but they most likely will find ways to resist and even sabotage the efforts if they do not fully buy in as owners of the change. Compliance is one thing, but acceptance is entirely different.

In my previous book, *The Power Of Or: Choosing And Doing What Matters Most*, I talk extensively about choices. I have concluded that choice can never truly be a mandate. Even if you take the approach that your employees must comply with the change you intend to implement, it still does not mean that they are without a choice. Now, the consequences of non-compliance may be too significant for the employee, and therefore, they go along with the change. In the end, they still have a choice.

I am not attempting to be cute with this unpacking of what choice is; I just want to emphasize the importance of understanding its role in the change process.

The point is that you cannot manage choices. You can influence how people think about the options they have and how they feel about the change.

So how do you minimize change being treated as a choice? How do you get people to do what you want them to do because they want to do it?

Well:

Start by making good decisions. Implement good changes. I am serious here. Introducing stupid-ass ideas will generate negative responses- plain and simple. Use logic and a thoughtful approach, and your acceptance rate of change will shoot way up.

Also, make people part of the process. That does not mean letting them dictate what the change is. It can look like you creating the guardrails for what the end product of change needs to look like and let them help you navigate. There are typically many decision points along the way of implementing change. Even though you may be the leader, it does not mean that you need to decide every aspect of the change.

I will talk about this more in a later chapter when I discuss resistance.

Think about the choices that you and the people in your organization have. Sometimes what does not seem to be a choice is only viewed that way because you have given up your right to choose. I know that is not fair- most people do not manage up in their organization. Many that do attempt it end up telling their story from the comfort of their couch.

Nonetheless, choice, when exercised, can be powerful.

I found myself in this situation while working as the chief

operating officer at Jamba Juice. From the first day, we talked a lot about change and a lot about choice. We were going through a business transformation, which is just a fancy term for the business was a train wreck.

Being in a 95% franchise store system, you learn that there is choice- choice by the owners. While there are some things mandated for franchisees to participate in per the agreement, there are also many areas in which they can opt-in or opt-out.

In the franchise environment, change becomes even more critical because of the presence of choice.

Sure, implementing change is hard enough in company-owned stores or with your direct employees, but it is a far more challenging endeavor with franchisees. And this is not because franchise owners are resistant or complicated, just the opposite. They are looking at the bottom line and the cash implications of every decision. They want only to do things that make good dollars sense and good common sense. As a franchisor, you have a responsibility to ensure that any change introduced checks both of those boxes.

While everything was a challenge in the Jamba Juice business model, we had to zero in on specific areas to fix. We examined every process and realized we were limited with resources to take on the problems we identified. We had to make choices. It came down to three priorities- Execute The Concept, Revolutionize The Brand, and Fix The Plumbing. In laymen's terms- operations, marketing, and IT.

No one can guarantee that there will be an easy choice or a clear and obvious choice, but as long as you have options, you have free will to choose. What we had to gauge is what action would demonstrate real change.

The physical store assets at Jamba were tired and dated, the computer systems and technology were at the end of their useful life or not fully utilized, the offerings were not healthful enough- not keeping up with new ingredients and food options, and overall marketing messaging was non-existent, especially on social media. And oh, if we were honest, the operation was not that strong either.

Enter our new leadership team, all new leadership team. Seven of us with a total of four years of Jamba Juice experience- I know, the numbers do not make sense.

We had all come from different industries and we all had our own ideas of what was most important to do. In the end, we had to align on choices.

Even when we developed a well-thought-out strategy, our greatest challenge was introducing it and implementing it amongst the franchise owners. Again, they have a greater degree of choice flexibility to accept or reject the change. To my point earlier, stupid-ass ideas will be rejected... and if I were them, I would have rejected some of the ideas that we proposed too.

Fortunately, that was not the case with all the ideas. We simply had tough decisions to make, and franchisees were in a position to look at their bottom line, all while attempting to understand our situation and the financial implications of our strategy. And oh, we were a publicly-traded company that needed to be private.

Listen, most of our propositions to transform the business were win-lose at best, and some were even lose-lose. Most of the easy win-win opportunities had long been exhausted by the previous leadership team, which landed us in this murky position. I am sure all good-intentioned leaders, as I know none of them personally, but while they were tinkering around with line extensions, the competition became sophisticated and left Jamba Juice behind in the health and wellness category.

We also learned that change is not just about development and implementation. It is also about diagnosis- we will get to that in a later chapter- and it is about choosing what to focus on.

When change is introduced and is not solving the most critical problems, you may have teams questioning the leadership, so choosing what to focus on is vital.

First, in operations, we had been selling company-owned stores in markets to franchisees in recent years. The implication of this was a narrative that franchisees were purchasing company-owned stores and then operating them better than the corporate structure. My operational senses told me that I should fact-check that. So, I did, and here is what I found:

I found that it was not totally true, nor was it totally false. On paper, many franchisees were purchasing company-owned stores and delivering a better bottom line profit in the first twelve months after the purchase. That part is true. However, year one is relatively easy as you can simply strip away costs from the store or even move some costs to overhead in your organization. What was also true is that the company-owned stores were not being operated very well before the sale to franchisees, so honestly, the results had nowhere to go but up.

However, on the key performance metrics that demonstrate the health of the business- mystery shops, customer service scores, and food safety audit scores- the franchise stores, by and large, went down across the board. So, for that, the narrative was false.

Telling some of the franchise owners and operators that they were running a lousy operation is not a message that you want to send, but one that had to be sent, nonetheless. The art is doing it and still maintaining good relationships.

Over six months, we changed vendors, changed frequency of auditing, and changed reporting. Mostly though, we changed how we measured success. High volume stores were no longer given carte blanche as being exceptional stores. The key metrics, the real health of the business, had to be up to standard.

This was a key in sharply turning around our financial results, and specifically our comp store sales, in a noticeably short period.

Most owners embraced the changes, and the narrative moved back to a reasonable place. Some owners did run better operations than company-owned stores, and some did not.

Anyway, the real test comes in year two and three when you

must cycle against the costs you pulled out of the business... and most of the owners knew that.

At the beginning of the next fiscal year, we introduced the new key performance metrics and new reporting. I had given the CEO a heads up that his phone would likely begin to ring when the new reports went out... and it did. However, I also shared with the CEO that if his phone begins to ring that it is a good thing- it means that the owners care.

Franchisees were immediately questioning the results- from the data source to the methodology for ranking. I was personally pleased to see the dialogue happening- I had struck a nerve. The competitive, operational nerve that lies in everyone, and it takes the right situation to bring it out- this was it. I recognized that part of the interaction around this change was that franchisees had never seen each other's results on a broad U.S. scale or the results of the company-operated stores.

This change opened up the door for best-practice sharing on a scale that the organization had not seen before. In the end, the changes made us stronger, not just in results but also in relationships. Also, franchisees had a choice in this regard as well- they could choose to participate and embrace the new change or be in denial and do what they always did. To their credit, almost all of them actively participated in the change.

Second, shifting to marketing- while choices may not have been plentiful, opinions certainly were. When it comes to marketing in a franchise environment, there is always a desire for more marketing, especially when sales trend the wrong way. Marketing usually becomes the lightning rod for the conversation about the franchisor not doing enough to drive sales as the reason for the sales gap. Not only were sales in decline when the new leadership team arrived, but the sales had also been trending negative year on year for several years.

The health and wellness space had become crowded, and we had lost market share to upstarts that provided more trendy options and shinier, new stores. Well, that is being kind. Jamba Juice had not innovated at all or kept up with the times, and other companies had passed them by. Yes, I am repeating this because sitting still in business usually means falling behind. There are many American business case studies of companies that are no longer around because of this very reason.

From a marketing perspective, though, for Jamba Juice, it was a Catch-22. The operation was not strong enough to garner the confidence to market the brand to drive customers back in. At the same time, we were not spending money on marketing, so even if the operations were good, we talked to the same customers. Dilemma.

In the end, the change needed in marketing was dramatic. During my time at Jamba, there were two different chief marketing officers with vastly different philosophies and approaches to marketing.

I recall a conversation that I had with an industry colleague after I had left Jamba Juice. There was a question about which chief marketing officer had the best approach to solving the brand identity challenges. My answer was both. Not both because I could not decide. No, one was extraordinarily strong at brand

and innovation; the other was exceptionally strong at research and design. The answer is both because we needed change in all four areas. Change that we could not afford, but change that we needed, nonetheless.

It was a frustrating space to attempt to implement change. We ran promotion after promotion and saw no growth in traffic or overall sales. We tested delivery, we launched catering, we even updated our app.

Only then could we step back and, my words not the chief marketing officer, see that we were just delivering improvement, not real change.

Real, sustainable change would require creativity- so, what did we do? We flew the entire leadership team to Boston for an innovation session, we partnered with operations engineers to help us signal something different in the design, and we ultimately built a Jamba Juice of the future, actually two versions- two versions that looked nothing like the current design, logo and all. That was change.

Real, sustainable change would also require participation. By and large, franchise owners were asking for a lot, but not willing to contribute much. It is a broad statement, and admittedly, it does not tell the whole story. Unfortunately, we had some franchisees who could not afford to participate more due to their current balance sheet and cash flow deficiencies. That was also a Catch-22. We needed to refresh stores and believe in the bet that updating the asset would attract new customers or re-attract lapsed customers.

One sobering reality about lapsed customers is that they are more challenging to acquire than bringing in new customers simply because they already have a negative view of the business that you must overcome... and Jamba Juice had many of those customers.

In the end, the choice was about whether franchisees would invest in the new Jamba. I left as that part of the story was being written with the sale of the company.

It was established that real, sustainable change would require investment. And that would not be the only area needing investment.

And finally, shifting to IT.

In IT, we had arguably more challenges than even what we were faced with within the operations or marketing space. While IT does not have the same defining metrics as operations to show successes or opportunities, there are still clear indicators of when you have a problem, like when you cannot take money from customers.

So, back to change is a choice. We knew that we needed to transform the business and needed to do so in the IT space. We needed to upgrade software in each store- company and franchise, we needed a new POS system across all stores, and we needed new back-office systems for the five percent of the system that was company stores. All expensive, all time-consuming, and all urgent. Literally, any of them could have been the right choice with the right argument in place.

When I arrived at Jamba, the team had already made the back-office systems the priority and had even begun the RFP (request for proposal) process to identify a vendor. Candidly, that was a bit self-serving as this would remedy company stores, but we were primarily a franchise system and growing in that direction.

As we juggled these three choices under new operations and IT leadership, I did a series of market visits with franchise owners-nine groups in nine weeks. I certainly heard about a lot of things that needed to be fixed. I cannot remember ever hearing the hue and cry in any other company that I heard regarding IT and the visible frustration of the inability to take currency from customers. That is game over for any retail business.

I returned to the headquarters as I wrapped up these visits and declared that we must make a different choice. We could no longer peddle the idea of a new back office system or think to the future about a new POS until we solved the issue of the day-taking money. The change needed was apparent, and the choice had to be upgrading the software to buy us more time. Even that was not going to be easy.

So, we aligned on our approach. We brought in a new chief information officer, whom I had worked with many years ago at Blockbuster. She was excellent! We joked about our Blockbuster days when the company attempted to crack the code on subscription model rentals.

For the task at hand, we knew that we had to re-order the priorities. Back office systems would fall to the third priority with POS needing to be focused on, but that meant getting an

RFP underway in an intermediate time frame. No doubt, the near-in focus had to be on upgrading the current POS software. It was painful to watch every day as many downloads did not get executed that we were attempting to do with virtually no resources. However, that was not nearly as painful as the impact on store managers and their employees as many were in tears due to their frustration. This had to be solved.

It eventually was solved. It took a lot of work by a tiny group of people, but they did it, and I was very thankful for them.

Just as marketing and operations have interplay on what drives sales the most, there is also an interplay between operations and IT.

In this case, solving the IT issues meant that we could remove that barrier and get people focused back on the operation. It was genuine concern from most store managers, but there was always a faction that used this as smoke-and-mirrors to deflect the focus away from their poor operation.

IT was yet another area that required financial participation from the franchise owners. Change is a choice- they all wanted this change, but they all did not choose to participate financially. It was quite a dilemma, and we worked vigorously to balance and share the financial burden required to get stores in compliance and to full capability to take currency.

Being faced with a high volume of choices, a high volume of difficult choices and preferences that no one would be happy with was all on display during my time at Jamba Juice. Admittedly, I did not love the process at the time, but I cannot tell you how valuable it has been, professionally and personally.

In our personal lives, we are faced with choices every day. When change is presented to us, we can go one way or the other. We can be change agents or change-averse. As I have heard it described, we can choose the "lesser of two evils." In each of these scenarios, the choice is not always about good or bad; it is about the situation.

Sometimes, just taking a moment to stop and think about the choices can yield clarity that seems elusive. We have been accustomed to making so many quick decisions and so many decisions in volume daily, that even stopping to take thirty seconds to think through a decision can seem like an eternity. Yet, it can reveal a new decision path.

This is true of my time with Jamba Juice. As our CEO would often say, "we are attempting to solve Gordian's Knot." The Gordian Knot is a metaphorical expression that means a complicated or unsolvable problem. There are many origins of the story of the term, including a tie to Alexander The Great, but all intimate an intractable problem solved only by "thinking outside the box." We had to do a lot of that.

Since that time, I have discovered a different energy level when making choices and making them confidently, almost borderline being too confident. But you know what, I will take that over indecision. Making tough choices has paved the way for making tough choices, at least for me.

I have found myself being more thoughtful about the choices that I make too. In particular, when I am faced with a choice that I may have to live with for a long time, I have put more emphasis on whether I am going to be satisfied or dissatisfied. I suppose you cannot always make the right choice, and inevitably I have found myself disappointed when I did not like the outcome. I can live with that as long as my choices do not leave me utterly dissatisfied.

CHAPTER 9:

Utter Dissatisfaction

This principle is straightforward. For real, sustainable change to occur, you must ultimately be dissatisfied with the current state. Without this level of dissatisfaction, it is likely that the consequences of changing are not dire enough to outweigh staying where you are.

Utter dissatisfaction is a far deeper feeling than just disappointment. You must have a disgust, a visceral reaction to the status quo.

The challenge is to do this without creating a crisis, a burning platform, or an ultimatum.

For many to become utterly dissatisfied, the consequence must become greater than the reward.

It is as simple as this example- I can remember early in my career attending a one-day leadership seminar when those were the thing to do. The speaker was great; the content was great;

the energy from others around me was great. I even walked out buying a book about what I just heard... and then, three weeks later, nothing. I was back to my old routines. Why? Perhaps it was artificial motivation. Someone else wanted the change for me, but apparently, I did not really want the change for myself. I was being sold on change, rather than a case being made for me to change... I just did not know that at the time.

In the end, though, I could not muster up enough internal disgust to say that I will no longer accept the status quo and do something different. Yes, it was all about what I did not do, not what someone else did or did not do.

Doing something different is an exceedingly tricky aspect of change- only you can make it happen. However, sometimes it is the emotion of being utterly dissatisfied that must show up and be the catalyst for change.

Utter dissatisfaction creates action. If it does not, then we are not talking about utter dissatisfaction.

Take, for example, someone who is significantly overweight. I do not mean like the former "Extreme Makeover" shows on television. No, I mean real, everyday people dealing with the challenge of excessive weight.

For those that have gone through significant weight loss, many have shared that there was that one moment- on the scale, looking in the mirror, a negative comment from someone, a reality-check diagnosis from a doctor. That something that created an I-have-had-enough moment. That is utter dissatisfaction.

Utter dissatisfaction could be applied to a relationship gone wrong, a challenge with a co-worker, a challenge with one of your children. Whatever the situation in life, when we reach utter dissatisfaction, we are not just determined that a change must occur, we are propelled to action.

In this chapter, I will walk through examples of utter dissatisfaction. I will then discuss some methods to manage utter dissatisfaction.

Let me start with this example:

I had a former co-worker, Carl, from many years ago that attempted to quit smoking on several different occasions. I considered us to be friends, but I would reflect in later years that one of the fundamental reasons that Carl and I did not become closer friends was because of his smoking- it was a hindrance to riding in the car together, to going out to lunch together, or doing anything together.

A gratuitous public service announcement- everyone should stop smoking if cigarettes have the power to kill you and, at the same time, kill relationships.

I had known Carl for years and understanding the depth of his struggle with smoking, I finally asked him one day, "why don't you just stop smoking?" As I have never smoked, I acknowledge that I do not fully understand the complexities of nicotine and the difficulty in stopping. His answer surprised me- he said, "I know that smoking is not good for me, but I don't care about what will happen thirty years from now. I will deal with it then, if I even live that long."

Wow!- I was fascinated by his response. Perhaps, it was because he was so matter-of-fact about it. Perhaps, because he was so calculated as to what his odds were, and apparently, he liked his odds in the current situation. Again, not understanding the mentality and, of course, addiction of a smoker, I could not wrap my mind around his response.

Maybe many of us think like Carl in the decisions that we make in our personal lives every day. On this day, the topic happened to be smoking, and the person happened to be Carl.

I had no comeback for Carl's response. I could only hope that there would be a moment sometime in the future that would change his view... for his sake and the sake of those that cared about him.

Carl and I both went on to work at other companies, and many years later, I ran into Carl, and we agreed to have dinner a couple of weeks later to catch up, and the topic of health and smoking came up. I was incredibly happy to hear that Carl had stopped smoking several years earlier. I could hear the pride in his voice as he spoke about his journey to quit smoking.

Of course, I could not resist the obvious question, so I asked, "how did you finally do it?"

Admittedly, I was not prepared for his response.

His son, now fifteen years old, was having severe respiratory problems and was at risk of having a lung removed at the age of twelve.

Carl took his son in to see a specialist, and they believed the root cause of his son's respiratory problem was exposure to... you guessed it- second-hand smoke over the years.

Of course, Carl's son did not smoke at the age of twelve, and none of Carl's friends or family smoked; there was literally no one in Carl's circle that had ever smoked... except for Carl.

I was speechless.

It was not a moment that I could disguise how I was feeling- the shock was all over my face, and it was apparent that Carl could see it.

I could also see Carl holding back the tears as he shared this story. While it had been some years since he stopped smoking, it was clear that the impact was still as real on that day as it was many years earlier. Carl knew that he could not undo the damage done to his son, and he had to live with that for the rest of his life.

In the end, Carl's utter dissatisfaction came from the fact that he had let his child down. In his eyes, he had committed the cardinal sin as a parent- he did not protect his child from all harm... In this situation, Carl was the one inflicting the damage. Carl even went as far as to share with me that his addiction had such a stronghold on him that there may have been no other situation that could have forced him to stop smoking.

As for Carl's son, while he could not get better, he was, at least, not getting any worse. The consequence of Carl's actions was evident every day in his son's health and physical limitations due to complications from emphysema.

I share this story for the context of this book, but I certainly hope that no one else must learn that lesson in the way that Carl did. For Carl:

To become utterly dissatisfied, the consequence had to become greater than the reward.

Again, utter dissatisfaction can be a catalyst for good change. Taking this utter dissatisfaction and turning it into positive energy is what best-in-class leaders do.

You see it in all facets of life. For example, someone who gets passed over for a promotion. Not just a promotion that they wanted, but one in which they appeared to be the obvious choice. That utter dissatisfaction can create an outcome that can be a motivation for a long time to come. That sounds personal, doesn't it? That is because it is. It is part of my story.

I can say that I have been a servant leader, a humble leader most of my life. However, there was a time when I was not. A time when I believed in "I" more than "we." I am not proud of that moment in time.

I was a senior director in the operations department. I had moved into the corporate office only a year earlier, and I had just completed a year-long store re-engineering project with external consultants. The overall endeavor was a success, and the consulting firm leaders lauded me for my participation in the project. The project had also given me exposure to our executive leadership team for the first time. I must admit, I was feeling great about my accomplishments. Too great.

Remember that word hubris that I spoke about earlier in the book? Hubris is usually attributed to organizations. The people equivalent of hubris is arrogance- that is what I had.

I was the shiny object, the "it" guy, the highest of the high potentials.

Shortly after the consulting engagement, I was asked by a former boss to take a role in the franchise department. I did not know much about franchising to that point in my career, and frankly, I did not want to know. I politely declined her opportunity.

This boss was someone I loved- she was the inspiration for much of my leadership development then and even now. She had a very dominant and persuasive personality. Most people did not tell her no. Even though I said no, she came back around- what a surprise. Her second attempt at a pitch was not asking; it was her explaining why this is good for me.

I would like to believe that I could have continued to tell her no, but that was probably not reality. I ultimately said yes to the role and accepted the position of senior director of operations. I accepted it because I trusted her.

I did not have much success in the first six months in the role, but that was my fault. I had chosen to do things the hard way, which in translation means my way.

She had warned me that relationships are the most critical aspect of a franchise environment. I heard her, but I apparently was not listening. I barreled right through that stop sign from the outset of the job as I was hellbent on demonstrating what I knew to all the franchise owners. After all, I just came out of a role where everyone loved me, even the consultants.

I can recall flying back to the headquarters after a market visit six months into the role, and my boss and I talked through the challenges that I was experiencing. She basically told me that I was the problem, and basically, she was right. I still recall that conversation many years later and appreciate it just as much now as I did then.

Nonetheless, while the first six months were bumpy, things got much better when I decided to act like an adult and listen to my boss, the franchise owners, and others. The job became extremely rewarding. I did learn a lesson about how critical relationships are when you begin a new role or begin at a new company.

After completing the first year in the role, I began to apply what I had learned and gained momentum. About eighteen months into the role, we decided to add a vice-president of franchise operations role. I was well-positioned and was excited about the possibility of getting the VP role. I had many people rooting for me internally, even some of the franchise owners weighed in on my behalf. As the senior director, it was the natural progression. The other senior director in the department led the field organization and had been in his role much less time than I had.

Franchise stores made up only 15% of the total stores in the system, so there was not much focus on the franchise stores. That is probably too understated. More appropriately stated, no one on the company-owned side of the business gave a shit about the franchise side. There, that is better.

The point of that is there were no ready-for-promotion-to-vice-president leaders that had any interest in coming over. That said, the role was mine... or so I thought.

I went to the VP "interview" with my boss. It felt like a formality. After the interview, the waiting began. A week passed, and then another week. As more time passed, doubt started to creep in, but my arrogance would override it each time. It had to be me.

And then it was not.
There was an ex-patriot at the VP level moving back to the U.S. business that needed a place to land. He landed in my spot. He took my VP job. At least that is what I told myself.

I began to rationalize the situation. He was already a vice president; how could I compete with that? He had been in franchising roles for much of his career; how could I compete with that? He was guaranteed a job back in the U.S. when his international stint was concluded; how could I compete with that?

The answer was that I could have been a better leader and been ready for the opportunity in a way that I could not be denied. I had not, and therefore, I crash-landed back to earth.

My utter dissatisfaction for not getting the job was further exacerbated by the fact that it was my boss's decision to bring in someone from the "outside." It felt like the ultimate act of betrayal. Yes, dramatic writing is my specialty, but I am not being dramatic here for effect- I was truly hurt.

The utter dissatisfaction from that experience motivated me for years to come. I became more driven than ever to become a vice-president. Probably driven for the wrong reasons, but driven, nonetheless.

The snub for the promotion caused me to reflect on my performance, my leadership shadow for the first time. I must admit, I did not like what I saw.

In reflection, not only was I utterly dissatisfied with not getting the role and utterly dissatisfied with my boss, I realized that I was utterly dissatisfied with myself... and that was a good thing.

I proceeded to work differently from that point on. For my final years with that company and into the next company, I took with me the value of relationships and listening and being a servant leader and being more aligned with my boss and understanding the emotional wake that I was leaving and becoming a student of my craft and taking nothing for granted and...

Without a doubt, the most challenging lesson that I have learned in my career. Without a doubt, the most important lesson that I have learned in my career.

Utter dissatisfaction will always cause you to show up differently going forward. It will also compel you to action... always.

Let me shift gears on this subject of utter dissatisfaction to discuss another example. Let us go back to a word that I mentioned in chapter seven that I said I would come back to later... legacy.

I was on a market visit many years ago with an experienced operations leader, Kim. At that time, Kim was a regional director and had many years of success in the role.

We visited a small market to conduct a roundtable with her district manager team and all market store managers.

We discussed legacies that day. Interesting, it was the first time I had ever had a conversation about legacies on a field visit.

Let me say more about legacies. A legacy can be a small thing. For example, you may be disgusted with the service that you receive at your local grocery store. As a result, you complain to the manager. When the problem was not resolved, you complained to the next level of management. To no avail- the issue is not resolved to your satisfaction. You vow to never shop there again, but over the next few months, you go back in. The location is too convenient not to try it again, but a poor service experience shows itself with every attempt.

That grocer has established a legacy with you... and it is not a good one. Conversely, if that same grocer resolves your issue, fixes it promptly, and exceeds your expected remedy in doing so, you likely become an advocate for the brand. The legacy that grocer has created becomes a story that you tell others. Although, we often share more negative service stories than positive service stories, you get the point.

On the other side of this, a legacy could be a huge thing- like you developed the cure for cancer. Whatever it is, make sure that it is the legacy that you want to have.

That brings me back to the regional director, Kim, and an example where legacy and utter dissatisfaction intersect.

I asked a relatively simple question of Kim- which was, what do you think your legacy is as a leader?

She thought about it for a moment and then deferred to her district manager team to answer for her. I felt that it was a leadership move that demonstrated confidence on her part and an understanding that your legacy is ultimately defined by others.

The district managers and a couple of store managers responded almost in unison with one word to describe the regional director's legacy- "floors."

Kim was floored by this response... pun intended.

For all of her contributions over the years, her legacy had been summarized with one word and not the word that she would have chosen- "floors." Utter dissatisfaction was all over her face. Not embarrassment, not anger, just this I-can't-believe-it-and-I-am-going-to-change-that-and-never-let-that-happen-again-look.

Of course, Kim did not want to be known for floors. To her credit, at that moment, she owned it. She even laughed about it, all the while boiling on the inside.

I am not sure what compelled me to ask that question on that day, but I am glad that I did.

Of course, I probed to understand how we got here.

It is simple. The district managers and store managers responded by sharing that this was her pet peeve. Kim could not and would not stand for dirty floors. So much so that she could not resist mentioning it on market visits, every market visit.

Part of the lesson learned is that what you focus on and talk about in stores is what your legacy becomes. You can talk all day about recognition, employee development, business acumen, and other priorities. Still, if those do not make it into the store visit conversation or are spoken of less consistently than floors, then floors it is- that is what is remembered.

Of course, Kim did not talk about floors that often after that day.

You can also flip this conversation on its side and talk about what happens when you land that legacy that you want- the one that people will talk about for years. However, we are talking about utter dissatisfaction here.

So, what is the breaking point? What makes you finally say that is it- I am utterly dissatisfied, and I must do something? Of course, you already know the answer to this- it depends. Honestly, only you know that answer for what exists in your life, personally or professionally.

We have discussed examples that led to utter dissatisfaction. So, let us now discuss some methods to manage and even eliminate utter dissatisfaction.

Here are a few tactics to take with you on your daily journey:

- Remember what caused your utter dissatisfaction- once you forget it and forget the emotion of it, the urgency of it, old behaviors are likely to return. Post it somewhere visible to you each day, make it the background image on your computer or phone, get it tattooed- whatever is necessary to keep it top-of-mind... every day.

- Post the utter dissatisfaction on social media or share it broadly with friends, family, or co-workers. Exporting it into the universe ensures that you cannot take it back- it forces you to now deal with the consequence of placing it in the public domain. As is said, you cannot put the toothpaste back into the tube. It puts you in a position where there is no turning back, and you are now on the hook to make the change you are after. Careful with this one, though, you better be sure you are ready.

- Put a lot of money towards the utter dissatisfaction. Whatever is proportionate to your earnings to feel like it is uncomfortably too much money. Most things that we spend a lot of money on, we only feel the value by using it or doing it. Well, except maybe expensive, unused timeshares- yeah, that one still hurts. You get the point here.

Let me be clear on one other point related to utter dissatisfaction. Utter dissatisfaction is not snapback change, meaning your dissatisfaction does not just dissipate, and you decide to revert back.

Remember, the change that I am discussing in this book is real, sustainable change. Going back to the initial state is what happens when you are just upset or disappointed.

This is why I am continuing to draw out a distinction here and use specific language- utter dissatisfaction. Change that I discussed earlier in the book that comes from a life-or-death situation may not be sustainable change. An example would be someone who begins having liver problems due to excessive alcohol consumption, stops when the health scare presents itself, and then begins to drink again when they believe they are "in the clear."

The person was not utterly dissatisfied, just mostly inconvenienced because something happened to them that disrupted their way of living.

In summary, utter dissatisfaction can be challenging, but when appropriately leveraged, it can be a catalyst for change. Part of managing through change is also being able to solve problems that will arise as you prepare for the change, while going through the change, and even as you are working to sustain the change.

These solutions largely determine the fate of the change and its long-term success.

However, solving problems is not enough to get you to the finish line on change. The process used to solve for the right solutions is also critical.

CHAPTER 10:

Solving For Solutions

Problem-solving and solving for solutions are not the same thing... and this is more than just wordplay.

Many leaders are good at identifying problems- what you need are leaders that can solve problems. Even beyond that, you need leaders that can solve for solutions.

Many times, we may be "writing prescriptions for illnesses that we do not have"- I love that quote. It is from a former colleague- an executive and long-term retailer. He would say that often around the boardroom table, and it served to be a marker in many conversations when we were off the track.

It is a strong metaphor. I am not sure that any of us would take medicine that we did not need to take. Yet, in the business world, we are often spending time solving things that are not even a problem, as in the Lean example earlier in the book.

There could be an unintended consequence when we attempt

to solve a problem that does not exist. We end up spending time on everything except the real issues, and, in line with the metaphor, we have misdiagnosed. We may also lose credibility with our team. This is my interpretation of his words.

Even if what we were trying to solve is a problem, it may not be the most critical problem, or at our best, we solved the problem without getting to the root cause.

Solving for solutions is about identifying all possible solutions and ultimately getting to the root cause. Solving for solutions is also about solving a problem in a way that prevents the same problem from occurring again.

Part of the philosophy of solving for solutions means working the situation backward from conventional thinking. What I mean is that many leaders and leadership philosophies have stated that you should start with the end in mind. There was a set of Seven Principles introduced many years ago that talked about this. It is not that it is wrong... it is just incomplete. Thinking about it differently, starting with the end in mind, could leave you selling yourself short. Why? The end in mind of today may not be the end in mind of tomorrow.

Solving for solutions is not that.

Solving for solutions is start at the beginning and work your way through to the end.

Let me explain.

During my tenure at Blockbuster, if you had asked any of us

what success looked like or where we wanted to be in five years or ten years as an organization, you would have likely heard something like: 'continue to be the leader in the industry and grow market share.' Actually, not that different than what you hear from many organizations who are front-runners in their industry.

This is classic starting with the end in mind. The answer is not wrong, but you effectively cap yourself on what success could look like. And that is what we did at Blockbuster. Not intentionally, but we determined our finish line with that statement. Effectively, the market, with all the emerging technology, caused the finish line to continue to move, and it ultimately left us short of reaching success. Ultimately, our definition of success was nowhere near the new finish line.

In this example, solving for solutions would be staying aggressive and working ourselves through each new industry ripple and recalibrating what success would look like. That would have resulted in a different response to subscription sales and, of course, a different reaction when Netflix came calling. It would have resulted in a more aggressive approach to vending machine testing- yes, we tested our own vending machines long before Redbox. It would have also resulted in a much more thoughtful approach to online and streaming services, and yes, we were testing our own Blockbuster channel.

With solving for solutions, the answer to the question of what success looked like or where we wanted to be in five years or ten years as an organization would have sounded something like this:

'We want to extend our business model to address new trends, and new consumer needs to remain relevant and remain the leader in our industry. We will stay aggressively committed to continuous improvement and invest in resources and structure to challenge our status quo. We have to believe there is a possibility that customers will engage with entertainment and movies in new ways in the future and we need to be at the forefront of those changes while maintaining a core business to fund the future. Being the leader in the industry, we see ourselves as our most significant competitive threat.'

That is looking at the situation differently.

Think about industries that have been developed and then completely disappeared in short order- much faster than even Blockbuster... like pagers.

This sounds like a good place to digress.

Depending on where you are from, pagers, or beepers, were the cool way of communicating in the early to mid-'90s. Cell phones had not become mainstream, and if you could afford to have one, you couldn't afford the minutes to talk on it or the physical workout to carry it around. So, pagers ruled.

So much so, by 1992, more than 2.9 million pagers were in use in the U.S. By 1996, Japan touted more than 10 million pagers in use. While some pagers are still in use in the U.S. and other countries for business industry-related purposes, they virtually disappeared in the U.S. by 2003- a very short life. Japan has completely shut down the radio signal used for pagers.

Pagers did solve a problem, a need, but did not find a way to evolve in the communication space.

Pagers were functional. They became standard-issue for doctors, and anyone of importance in the business world found the need to carry a pager.

Pagers eventually became more pop culture than functional. They found their way into the rap industry and became a status symbol.

So then, what happened to pagers? Shortsightedness. Those in the industry did not solve for solutions.

Ultimately, pagers became irrelevant and inconvenient- two things you never want to become in the business space.

Pagers became irrelevant because the functionality was so limited. Solving for solutions may have led to the pager industry merging with mobile phone developers to add a "window" on the pager to display more than just numbers- perhaps messages, and even videos in the future. Another missed opportunity was to turn the radio signal into a cellular signal to allow you to "answer" the pager. Additionally, the speaker could have been turned into a two-way speaker for communication.

I know it is easy to play Monday morning quarterback now but considering what was already available in technology at that time, even if it was just military-grade approved and used, it at least gave some insight into the future possibilities.

Pagers became inconvenient because you had to pull off to the side of the road to use a payphone to call the person back, based on the number listed on the pager. Tedious. That behavior was acceptable for a while, but mostly because people simply had no other choice. Those in the pager industry knew that but things were going so well so there was no compelling reason to change. At some point, though, the two-way usage of a cell phone was worth the incremental cost, and pagers were unceremoniously ushered out of our lives. Ultimately, cell phones were to pagers what UBER was to the taxi services. Everyone can speak of some awful taxi experience they had over the years- no answer, no callback, late to pick up, dirty car interiors filled with smoke. But we had no choice. UBER capitalized on the massive customer dissatisfaction.

Pagers created enough customer experience dissatisfaction that users would likely migrate to the newest technology that would come next, any technology... and they did. The pager industry disappeared faster than you can say, Houdini.

I am not sure of any business models that have survived being both irrelevant and inconvenient.

One more story about Blockbuster.

To put a fine point on the abject failure that Blockbuster has been in the technology space and failing to solve for solutions, I will share this.

My daughter, Nymera, and I took a trip to Portland last year. We were long overdue for a father-daughter trip, and so I asked her to name a few cities that she was interested in us visiting together. After some thought, her list was narrowed down to three cities- New York, New Orleans, and Portland.

My first response was to skip New York for now. We had been to New York in the past few years and had an amazing time and, although New York never gets old, we can do that another time.

Second, I also recommended that we not go to New Orleans- too many reasons not to visit outweighed the reasons to visit. There is an incredible amount of history in the city, which is why she recommended it; however, the last few years have not been kind to the city. Sorry to my Louisiana friends- I lived in New Orleans pre-Katrina, and the city had plenty of issues even then.

So, we were left with Portland. Even though it was by default, I thought Portland was perfect! I mean, we lived in Austin, and Portland has been called Austin's sister city with the 'Keep It Weird' moniker- minus the traffic.

While I had been to Portland a few times over the years for work- well, they were just that, work trips. I never got to explore the city at all. I got excited when I saw how excited she was about going to Portland. Our trip to Portland was on for a few weeks out.

It was a very relaxing trip. Honestly, the most stressful part of the journey was coming within seconds of having the plane doors close on us and missing the flight.

We spent five days there and had a wonderful time. Since

Nymera is very much organized and planful like me, we already had our prepared list of things to do. We did a lot of hiking and we did everything else that there was to do. We visited all the usual suspects- the Rose Garden, the Oregon Zoo, the Grotto, Multnomah Falls, Voodoo Doughnuts, and the Pittock Mansion, to name a few.

Ironically, one of the highlights of our trip was the one item that was not even on our list until we got to town. We saw a few attractions the first evening that we landed in Portland, and as we were arriving at the hotel, I asked my daughter, "are you interested in going to Bend, Oregon while we are here?" Nymera replied, "what is in Bend, Oregon?" I quickly responded with measured excitement, "the last Blockbuster Video on earth." Before I could even finish the sentence, Nymera said, "I'm in!"

We decided to drive three and a half hours south to Bend, Oregon. Yes, there is a Blockbuster Video in operation- only one Blockbuster in the world is in business, and it is in Bend, Oregon. Ken Tisher owns it, and he has no intention to close the store, and why should he? The store is busy and getting busier with all the press that it has received since the second to last Blockbuster store in the world closed in Australia. I certainly hope that it is still open at the time of this book being published.

So, Nymera and I made the trek from Portland down to Bend, Oregon. It is one of the most breathtaking drives with state parks and streams as far as the eye can see, and oh, waterfalls. They were all tempting us to stop, but nothing would distract us from our destination.

Perhaps, another day or two added to our trip, and we would have been seduced to stop and enjoy the journey to Bend even more.

We knew that we were in Bend even before we arrived at Blockbuster. The town had a feeling of a slower pace- we even had attendants pump our gas at the convenience store. I would come to learn that it is a state law, but nonetheless, it fit the speed of Bend and what we were feeling.

The anticipation was building as we were getting closer to the store. I was so excited as we approached the Blockbuster location that I took a snapshot of the map on my phone, showing our proximity to the store- it was surreal.

I can only remember feeling that way one other time being that close to a landmark on the GPS, and that was when I was at the White House. With all due respect to the White House, this was Blockbuster Video. I know that may sound dramatic to some, but Blockbuster is a piece of Americana that we will never see again. To see it fading, but with an opportunity to see it before it was gone, was pretty special.

As we pulled into the parking lot of Blockbuster, we were met with a colossal Blockbuster ticket sign that was far too big for this location, but hey, when you are the last of anything, you can have any sign that you want.

I believe our silence told the story. I was speechless, and I do not think my daughter said anything to me, and, if she did, I do not remember what she said. To add a bit more perspective, there may not be another 23-year-old anywhere in the country with the reverence for Blockbuster that my daughter has. I mean, she literally grew up on Blockbuster and movies. She can remember browsing the aisles of Blockbuster during her elementary years. She still has a VCR- who at her age does that?

We approached the doors of the store. From the outside, everything looked just as we remembered it. We went inside, and everything looked just as we remembered it- everything.

It was eerie- not eerie in a bad way. Time had stood still in this store. The new release wall was the same; the POS (point-of-sale) was the same; the concession items were the same... wait, the POS being the same was unbelievable. The POS was outdated back then; I honestly could not believe that it still worked. Even the rental terms were the same, and they got it right!- $3 for Three Days and a daily late fee of 99 cents. That was fair... and yes, that made sense.

The store was still using its Project Store cart. To explain, it was a cart that we designed to help re-shelve movies, but to go a step further, the cart would also be functional for other tasks such as movie markdowns and changing signage. The cart seemed so amazing at the time, and now it looked as simple and weathered as the feeling of Bend, Oregon. Broadly, Project Store was part of a re-engineering project that I led working with McKinsey- sixteen years earlier! I did not believe the carts would last for one year, and here it was still in use.

The rental locks to lock the DVDs inside the amarays and the synopsis on the movies were the same. Oh, let me stop there- I am getting too far into video store vernacular. The term amaray, which is a DVD cover, is not even recognized now in many dictionary listings. That tells you how far back in time this is.

The store was filled with movie memorabilia- very impressive artifacts that the owner had likely collected from studios and vendors over the years. Yes, I am using the word artifacts to describe elements of a modern-day business.

What was most fascinating about our visit was that the interactions at the register were exactly the same as twenty years earlier! We observed a customer walk up and it sounded like this:

> Employee- "Hello, you have a $2 balance on your account."
>
> Customer- "What was it for?"
>
> Employee- "It was for Bohemian Rhapsody."
>
> Customer- "Oh, we returned that two days ago in the drop box."
>
> Employee- "Do you know around what time?"
>
> Customer- "It was around 9:00 pm."
>
> Employee- "Okay, I will recheck our wall. I will take the $2 fee off for you this time."
>
> Customer- "Thank you."

This was precisely what the conversation sounded like twenty years ago. We were truly transported back in time.

We walked around for a couple of hours just taking it all in, and ultimately, we bought one of everything that we could. The store understood its relevance globally and had begun selling merchandise that identified them as the last Blockbuster on earth. Honestly, we were disappointed that they did not have more to buy than what they had at that time.

Now that I have taken you down memory lane let me get back to why we are here in this chapter- to talk about solving for solutions.

A few takeaways from this story:

Again, this story emphasizes the abject failure that Blockbuster has been in the technology space. After all these years, there were still no changes, especially in technology.

It also represents the fact that sometimes solutions even show up on our doorstep, as in the case of Netflix- imagine how powerful that partnership could have been today. No matter, if we are not looking for those solutions or are resistant to them (see hubris), we can miss the moment.

Of course, this is a compressed timeline when telling a story. In reality, there were many years, many opportunities, and many reasons for Blockbuster to solve the root cause when problems surfaced in the business model- not only the subscription, vending machine, and ultimately streaming service models, but even considering drive-thru, delivery, and other new convenience aspects. And of course, a better solution to solving the late fee dilemma.

Let me share one last thing about our Blockbuster visit. To be clear, the gaps that I described are not a reflection of the owner of this store- the owner is a wonderful human being and has represented the Blockbuster brand well for at least the twenty-five years or so that I have known of him. The collapse reflected the parent company offering nothing in the way of evolution through to the bankruptcy in 2010.

So, back to solving for solutions.

Beginning with the end in mind does not optimize performance. It can lock you into a pre-determined belief as to what the optimal result can be.

Even when we are specific about our aspirations, beginning with the end in mind is still a potentially limiting approach. For example, we inherently know that most problems that need to be solved do not have a "silver bullet" solution, and yet, there are times that we may stop with the first solution without considering how significant the impact could be from a comprehensive set of solutions.

There are two things to consider here.

The solution needed to create real change can come from several different stimuli around you- fear, consequence, reward, etc. No matter, the solutions required to make real change must be rooted in solving the right problem and solving it sustainably, unless you like to re-do work.

Solving for solutions also means challenging your team to think about what is possible if everyone contributed to their maximum.

It may require the team to identify the weak link on the team... let me rephrase that, it may require the team to call out the weak link on the team- most normal functioning teams almost always have team members that already know who the weak link is- they are usually just waiting on the leader to do something about it... a topic for another time.

Solving for solutions may also require you as a leader to approach your teams differently.

For example, evaluating how much you are doing for your teams. Many leaders say that they want participation from their team. In reality, leaders may find themselves dictating direction to their teams and doing most of the talking, stymying the opportunity for team problem-solving.

Creating the space to allow feedback from your team and asking them critical questions about the state of affairs could reveal key problems to solve and even yield solutions.

In summary, solving for solutions requires a number of actions to occur:

- Starting at the beginning and working your way through to the end
- Solving a problem in a way that prevents the same problem from occurring again
- Identifying all possible solutions to get to the root cause

- Identifying solutions that will allow real, sustainable change to occur
- Challenging your team to think about what is possible if everyone contributed to their maximum

Solving for solutions is not as much process as you may think. It requires asking the right questions to spark the problem-solving process and ultimately getting the team to generate solutions.

One aspect of arriving at real solutions to problems is gaining clarity.

CHAPTER 11:

For The Sake Of Clarity

So, let me talk about clarity. Clarity is the quality of being straightforward and easy to understand. Clarity is the quality of being easy to see or hear. Clarity is also the ability to think clearly and not be confused.

Generally, when a person says that they need more clarity, it can be translated as "I don't understand."

Because clarity is essential to the change process, someone who asks for clarity could be actively working through the change and asking for clarity ensures that they understand what is coming or what is being asked of them. Asking for clarity can also be an approach to buying more time as you move towards accepting the change.

However, if you listen closely, there are times when:

A person that says that they need more clarity can be translated as "I don't agree with you."

Now, you may contend that this is a negative few of a simple request for more information. You could be right; however, we live in a passive-aggressive world, and we are challenged more than ever as leaders, and even in our personal lives, to read between the lines.

It is easy in our daily interactions to be misunderstood or taken out of context. Particularly given how much of our conversations have been deferred to written communication through email, texts, and social media. We are not even using words to communicate anymore, but I will not rant about that right now. Perhaps, I should use the mad emoji face to make that point. Anyway...

All of this makes getting to clarity even more critical, but also even more difficult.

I am reminded of a leader I worked with years ago who ended almost every sentence with the same phrase, 'do you understand?' That simple question required a response of some kind and gave him a sense of how clear he was in his communication based on the other person's response.

Of course, I do not recommend that in all daily communication, as it could come across as robotic or "skilled" rather than a natural communication style.

It is often said, though, "In communication, seek understanding, not agreement." That may be acceptable in communication; however, that looks different in the space of change. With real, sustainable change, you need to get to understanding <u>and</u>

agreement for the change to occur. That said, understanding leads to agreement, so understanding needs to happen first-enter clarity.

Nonetheless, there needs to be a recognition that clarity can be a barrier to implementing real change in your organization or personal life.

The questions you ask of the person who says that they need more clarity are critical to implementing change.

Here are some starter questions for your consideration:

- What part of the change do you not understand?
- What part of the change do you not agree with?
- Where do you lack clarity about your role in the change?
- What can I do to make the change more acceptable?

These are very straightforward, introductory questions. You can learn a lot based on the responses back to you.

To go further, here are some additional questions to ask:

- In what way is this change different than what you were expecting?
- What is it about the change that seems irrational or illogical?
- Tell me about your level of resistance towards the change?

These questions have a bit more specificity to them and may help you better understand the clarity gap. However, anyone with nefarious intentions may not give you a straight answer.

I will admit that there is some risk in asking these questions or asking any questions to someone seeking clarity. Your approach is critical because you do not want to open the window for others to believe that they can alter the change that is coming.

Now, let me tie clarity back to a topic from earlier in the book- bias. When clarity concerns arise, one of the challenges is that two people could be given the same information. Still, with different filters based on their own biases, those same two people could hear completely different messages.

Yes, I believe it is true that sometimes we hear what we want to hear, but bias that leads to a lack of clarity is much more than that. It is a selective process to filter out information that does not agree with your belief system, which means you could miss critical change information. Again, that is how strong biases are.

Beyond your own bias, the better you know those you are leading through the change, or that you are going through the change with, the greater the likelihood of you identifying a clarity gap. Understanding why people do what they do may not get you to the finish line related to clarity, but it can help you gain alignment.

I worked with an attorney many years ago in one of my early director roles. Honestly, we just could not agree on anything. I felt like she had it out for me. Every situation that I presented to her, the answer was always no.

After about a year of working together, we were traveling to a conference to give presentations. When we arrived at the hotel, we learned that the meeting was about two hours behind on the agenda. It left the two of us sitting in the hotel lobby waiting. We literally had to talk to each other to break the awkwardness of our already awkward relationship. It ended up being one of the most important conversations that I have had.

What I learned about her family and upbringing was interesting. She grew up in a small town and went to school, K-12, with all the same kids. She even went to law school with the same kids. Her parents were ultra-conservative. Net result, she had been sheltered in a way that I could not comprehend, even though she was operating in a broad general counsel role.

This conversation helped me gain clarity as to why she made decisions the way she did. Her biases were formed early and hard-coded and was not a slight at me or anyone else.

My takeaway was that she had good intentions, but her perspective was different than mine.

Now, many factors can lead people to need clarity, so I believe the default position as a leader should be that everyone has good intentions... and biases.

What about when it is someone being passive-aggressive and does not believe in the change or direction? How should you handle that?

Well, that is an entirely different situation- see the word nefarious I mentioned earlier in this chapter. I will say you should respond directly. Anytime there is an attempt to derail the change process, you should take it seriously and invest the time to address it head-on.

Clarity is not just a matter of perspective; it is a matter of purpose and intention.

Clarity is too critical to the change process to overlook. You have a responsibility as a leader to ensure that everyone understands the change, but you also must ensure that everyone has good intentions about the change. Some will hide behind clarity, and when the shit hits the fan, they will simply say, I did not know, or I thought you meant...

I do not mean to mark clarity as more likely to be negative than positive. However, I believe the collective teachings around the word clarity have always been more of innocence and seeking information, almost ignoring the sinister aspect of it.

I will stop here and go back to a term that I mentioned very casually a couple of minutes ago... passive-aggressive.

So, what is passive-aggressive behavior? In short, passive-aggressiveness is anger and hostility. It is also an attempt to "get away with something" by disguising it and flashing an innocence when caught.

I will spend time on this topic because clarity can be incredibly elusive when you do not even know what the other person is saying and what the other person wants.

The passive-aggressive person is a moving target. Try shooting a basketball at a goal that moves around- pretty hard to be successful.

Passive-aggressive behavior is somewhat of an illusion, like a magic trick. You see it in the competitive co-worker who would never confront you directly but conveniently leaves your name off an email about an important decision. You know something just happened, you have been tricked, but you cannot prove it.

Passive-aggression is more than just a habit. Some experts believe that it qualifies as a full-blown personality disorder, like narcissism or paranoia. There is also consistent alignment about the characteristics of passive-aggression: deliberate inefficiency, avoidance of responsibility, and a refusal to state needs or concerns directly.

Passive-aggressiveness comes in varying degrees, though, which means there are even more characteristics to look for. For example:

The passive-aggressive person leaves things undone. Passive-aggressors are champions of the almost complete job: the laundry that is washed but does not get folded; The dishes that get washed, but not dried. They generally leave just little enough undone that you ultimately decide to do it yourself. Clever.

And oh, the passive-aggressive person is a master apologist. They apologize so often that they do not realize how often they say I am sorry throughout the day. I believe some of you just had a lightbulb moment. Hopefully, not in reflection of yourself, but I know you just thought of someone that says I am sorry all the time. Well, I am not going to label them, but maybe you should. This behavior can prevent change from occurring. No words create "back-away behavior" like someone saying I am sorry. To the point that you may begin apologizing for something you did not even do. Also, clever.

The passive-aggressive person is notorious for running late. This person may resent having to attend a meeting, so they wander in twenty minutes late with a mystified expression that says, why are you all here already? The behavior is occasionally deliberate, sometimes subconscious, and always infuriatingly effective.

The passive-aggressive person also takes compliments and turns them into something else. Here are some nice compliments: "Great haircut!" or "Terrific lasagna!" Here are some less nice compliments: "Great haircut – I used to get the same one back in college," or "Terrific lasagna- the spices stand out." If you are not sure which kind of compliment you have gotten, pay attention to your responses: If you feel like saying "thank you," you have probably gotten a good compliment. However, if you feel like punching them in the mouth...

The passive-aggressive person is also the master of the veiled insult. The social expectations under which the rest of us live does not apply to passive-aggressors. The disguised insult typically comes in the form of a "but" clause. Things like, "I don't want to sound mean, but..." "I hope you don't think I am being harsh, but...", after which they say something mean, insensitive or judgmental. You should hold up a hand and halt the conversation before the passive-aggressive person in your life gets past the comma because you will likely not be happy with what comes next. That said, do not be surprised if the passive-aggressive person plows right through that stop sign.

Passive-aggression is all nuance. You do not have to do much to turn something positive into something negative. I know it seems tiring reading about this behavior, but for some, it is the only way to live.

A passive-aggressive person can drive you crazy because, at times, this behavior works in reverse. What I mean is that the lack of clarity may not be with the passive-aggressive person, but instead with the receiver of the communication. Let me say it more straightforward- the person on the receiving end of this communication does not know what the hell the passive-aggressive person is trying to say.

It is so much easier when someone simply tells you what they want, and in the case of conflict, what it is that they do not like. The art of conversation should not require that you have a master's degree in psychology. To the passive-aggressive person, though, this shrouded communication can give the illusion they have passed on their concern, not realizing that they have likely made the situation worse.

I need to go more in-depth on this. To be clear, passive-aggressive behavior is sinister. The NYU Medical Center defines a passive-aggressive individual as someone who "may appear to comply or act appropriately, but actually behaves negatively and passively resists."

This is why this is so important to understand as part of clarity and how it rolls up to the change process. This behavior is sometimes so veiled that you could miss it and not know why your change did not stick... and this was the reason.

It is difficult to tell how often people intentionally set out to be passive-aggressive. There could be environmental factors that cause this behavior.

Sometimes, this behavior results from a societal constraint that limited their freedom of expression, like being the target of gender bias, homophobia, or some other type of discrimination.

There are times when this behavior begins closer to home-translation, parental behavior. Children watch and mentally file away everything that their parents do. It is not a stretch that a passive-aggressive person has a passive-aggressive parent.

Listen, I know I am painting a one-sided, pessimistic view of passive-aggressive behavior. I do not form any opinions without some rationale and experience... and bias. This bias, though, can help you avoid pitfalls. In this case, it is simple: Passive-aggressive behavior is so damaging that it leads to an erosion of clarity.

Communication is intended to drive more clarity, not create the need for more, but that is what passive-aggression can do.

I spent some time thinking about passive-aggression and word association. I wrote down all the words that could represent this behavior:

Backstabbing. Mixed messages. Deliberate button-pushing.

Procrastination. Stalling. Withholding information. Denying personal responsibility. Excuse-making. Blaming. Broken promises. Resistance. Stubbornness. Rigidity. Avoidance. Inefficiency. Exaggeration. Gossip. Sarcasm. Veiled hostile joking. Repetitive teasing. Habitual criticism of ideas. Social exclusion. Neglect. Victimhood. Dependency.

Okay, I feel better now that I have got that off my chest. Passive-aggression is as opposite to clarity as any behavior. Whether you are leading the change or leading others through the change, this behavior will slow you down; the only question is how much. That is passive-aggression.

Broadly, leadership has been described as being able to see around the corner. If there is any truth to that, then the most effective leaders will be prepared for anything coming around the corner... including passive-aggressive behavior. They will anticipate and outthink others around them and consider all outcomes- good and bad. They will identify the intention of clarity.

As long as you remember that clarity cuts both ways, you should be able to prepare yourself for any outcome.

Other elements become offshoots of clarity, one being silos. When people disagree with the information presented, a lack of clarity, they sometimes seek silos.

Let us explore silos.

A silo is a system, process, or department that operates in

isolation from others. Interesting that the first four letters of the word isolation spell the word silo. My apologies, my brain works like that.

Silo is a bad word in the halls of any organization. Even the mention of the word means that silos likely exist and have existed for some time in your business. Those that utter the word silo share it to signal a dog whistle to others in the organization, likely senior management, that people are not playing well together. However, it is not always accompanied by any specifics... and that is usually intentional. I know- cynical.

Many years ago, while I was working at Starbucks, I spent most of my time working in the field. However, the last few years were spent largely in the halls of the office in Seattle. During my time at Starbucks, we had many conversations about silos. After working in Seattle, I got it. We were working on separate floors with almost 4,000 employees at the time. It was hard to keep everyone informed and aligned to the priorities, let alone ensure that cross-functional relationships were being built and utilized to drive work. Of course, there was also the age-old challenge of headquarters versus the field, and each questioning whether the other one understood what the other one was doing.

After leaving Starbucks, I went to work for Jamba Juice in their headquarters. Early in my time there, I conducted an assimilation meeting- an opportunity for the team to get to know me as the new leader and for me to get to know them. Jamba was an asset-light model mostly supporting franchisees, so we were much, much leaner than Starbucks or even other companies our size. We had about 80 people working in our office, supporting 850 stores across the country. We had a slightly L-shaped office on the 7th floor with about 80% of our staff and the remaining 20% of staff on the first floor.

During this assimilation meeting, someone mentioned that one of the challenges in the office was that silos existed- no specifics, of course. At first, I thought that they were joking but quickly learned that it was no joke. I could only answer this one way. My response was swift and direct, "I mean, I can walk from my office on one end of the floor to where the chief marketing officer sits on the other end of the floor in about twenty-five seconds. How could we have silos?"

Silence. Perhaps, that was due to my response. It was one of the few moments in a business setting over the years, where I responded with a somewhat insensitive answer. It was a genuine response, though- I just did not see how it was possible in a company headquarters the size of ours.

As with all questions, I learn something. In this case, it was that silos are all relative to scale. You could have a department of five people, and if two are left out of the conversation loop, those two could believe that there is a silo. The only difference is we do not often use the word silo in that context- we call that a clique.

Relative to this conversation, silos can be a result of a lack of clarity. As humans, we often avoid what we do not understand. When that occurs in a work setting, we simply break off and create our own workgroup of comfort... one that is not anywhere on the corporate org chart.

So, silos and cliques are a watch-out. While I generally believe in positive intentions, a person who says that they need more clarity can be translated as "I don't agree with you."

If I were you, I would go and ask people on your team the question. Not if there are silos, but where are the silos. Do not be surprised if they do not look you in the eyes when they answer. No one wants to be the snitch... or they could very well be the leader of the silo. If you do not ask, you will never know.

Keeping balance here, I will jump back to an earlier point- clarity can also be someone buying time while they are processing the change.

This is also important not to ignore, but equally important not to judge. The timeline to adopt change is a slippery slope. Pressing people too hard to accept the change may turn them away from the change altogether... and they may have been so close to accepting it. If you do not press hard enough, those who are change-averse may take full advantage of it by stalling and delaying their acceptance of change. Again, this could cut both ways- they need more time, and if you give it to them, they will take it. On the other hand, it is the ultimate distraction tactic. To the point that the change-averse person is hoping that the longer they can hold out, they may get what they want to see happen- nothing, no change at all, and the change goes away.

One more angle on clarity. Be careful of the questions that someone seeking clarity is asking you. We often refer to this as "flipping the script."

Questions like, "Are you sure?" Are you sure? You are the one leading the change. Asking for clarity does not mean that you give up control of the change process. Watch out; this is a potential trap.

In the final analysis on this topic, asking for clarity usually yields something positive... with caveats, of course. You must look out for the deliberate attempts to derail the change using clarity as the cover, and you must ask the right questions to help those who are lost in the change process. One of those positives is someone who cares enough to ask the question to get the change right. No level of cynicism can override care.

After all, caring means that you are demonstrating behaviors like empathy and compassion.

CHAPTER *12:*

Empathy And Compassion

This chapter may not seem to fit in with the change process. Let me explain why it does.

When change happens, and emotions appear, the need for a different approach emerges.

If you want to effect real change inside others, do not use brute force- connect with their emotions. Use empathy and compassion.

It is not that you must demonstrate empathy and compassion as a leader; you should want to. This chapter is about appealing to the senses. It is about showing that you are a human being and not a robot. This is serious because many people think of their leaders as not being like them. That is a fatal flaw of leadership, and that flaw sits squarely with the leader, not with the people they are leading.

Let me start with this: Empathy and compassion are not the

same. However, I do believe that it is important to talk about the two of them together.

How you show up for others in their time of change is critical. Okay, now I am going to argue a bit against my own ideology here. What do you suppose happens when you demonstrate empathy or compassion when it relates to change you are looking to implement in your own life? Interestingly, it may not work so well. It may actually prevent you from implementing the change due to these emotions creating a victim mentality or even doubt about whether you can go through with the change. You may be left unmotivated even to engage if you allow these words to creep into personal change.

I am drawing this distinction here because, like most things in life, the use of emotions is situational, and these particular emotions related to change need to be used situationally.

To bring closure to this point, while empathy and compassion may not help personal change, they can be incredibly impactful in a leadership role leading change.

Empathy and compassion are words that many use interchangeably. It is understandable as these words are similar and, therefore, can be confusing. The headline on each of these can be described this way:

- Empathy is that you feel what another person is feeling.
- Compassion is the willingness to take action to relieve the person's suffering.

So, immediately you can parse compassion as more action-oriented than empathy.

Let me start by talking about how to think about empathy and compassion separately by going deeper into the definitions.

Take empathy first.

Empathy is the action of vicariously understanding the feelings and experience without having those feelings and experience fully communicated in an objectively explicit manner.

Empathy is viscerally feeling what another feels. Research has defined what are called "mirror neurons," so empathy may arise automatically when you witness someone in pain.

Let me shift to compassion.

Compassion takes empathy a step further. When you are compassionate, you feel the pain of another, or you recognize that the person is in pain, and then you do your best to alleviate the person's suffering from that situation.

Empathy vs. Compassion

An important distinction between feeling empathy and compassion is how they can affect your overall well-being.

Empathy can have an adverse effect on you emotionally. Compassion, however, is a renewable resource. When you can feel empathy for the other person but then extend a hand to alleviate someone's pain, you are less likely to burn out.

So why did I take you down this rambling road to discuss and contrast these emotions?

Because of compassion. Compassion is critical to the change process, and compassion compels you to take action.

When you are implementing change that involves others, and emotions are involved too, it is an exceptionally fine line as to whether you coach them or counsel them. Do not push hard enough, and the change does not happen. Push too hard, and the person's emotions will likely tip them over and, if the change does happen, it will be all compliance-driven.

There is no way to have full visibility to all elements as you lead change. However, you do have a responsibility to show empathy when you do know. More importantly, you have a responsibility to demonstrate compassion when you are in a position to do so.

For example, you could have an employee that comes to you and says that they are having an issue with another co-worker. The situation has escalated to the point that they can no longer work together, at least from the vantage point of the employee that came to you. As opposed to looking at the situation as conflict management and taking corrective action with one or both, compassion is taking action to move one of the two employees to a different workgroup and allowing them both to continue to grow and hopefully learn from the situation and thrive.

There is one advantage of being a leader that does not often get talked about- positional power. Positional power is literally compassion on steroids. Let me digress and explain why.

At one point in my career, I had a leader who would always contrast positional power and personal power. The narrative was this: personal power was always described as the positive, preferred path, and positional power was always portrayed as wrong. Let me expand on this.

Personal power was about taking the time to build relationships, which, in turn, would build trust. With that trust, you could lead people through inspiration and get people to do what you wanted or needed them to do. Sounds great, and I was always aligned to the belief, and I am still aligned to that belief. Inspiration is in the highest echelon of behaviors demonstrated by great leaders.

Pivoting to positional power. Positional power was always presented as misusing power and utilizing the direct-and-tell approach of getting work done. People will do it, but reluctantly, only garnering compliance.

The principle seemed logically sound, and I never challenged it until many years later. Since that time, I have come to shape a vastly different view of positional power, and that is that positional power has a side to it that is not negative at all. Instead:

Positional power allows you to do things for people that they cannot do for themselves.

I can recall market visits many years ago as a senior vice-president.

We would arrive at a store where the air conditioning may have been broken, or critical supplies needed for the store to operate had not been shipped. With one call, I could make it happen. It was not always about what the district manager, regional director, or regional vice-president were or were not doing... it was positional power. I saw this scenario play out over and over again throughout the years. Unfortunately, many people in organizations are not compelled to take action until they feel threatened by someone at a level that can impact their job. Not ideal, but this is real-world stuff. I suppose this can happen in your personal life with people that you believe can impact the decisions that you make.

For me, I never focused on the abusive side of positional power, but I acknowledge that there clearly can be one. I instead changed my view to look at how it could be helpful. I also looked at it through the lens of empathy, but it was compassion that compelled me to action. I realized that I could do something about situations that were brought to me. I have a couple of stories to share to demonstrate how compassion showed up for me as a leader and helped me to be more effective at change management. It also brought inspiration to the forefront for me as a leader.

Many years ago, I was in a vice-president role, and my wife was friends with a teacher that had taught our son in elementary school. That teacher had a daughter that worked in one of the stores that I was responsible for. Through my wife, it had been passed on to me that the daughter- I will call her Rose- was having a very tough time in her personal life. I would have never intervened, but this situation landed in my lap.

As the story goes, Rose was twenty years old and living with her boyfriend, attempting to make it independently as an adult. One day, the boyfriend disappeared- ending the relationship with no warning. He took the car, the pet, he even took her bicycle that she rode to work. For some reason, the word jerk always comes to mind when I retell this story. You hear stories like this, but you do not always hear about them up close and personal. If karma is truly real, I cannot imagine what his comeuppance will be.

I was dumbfounded, and the only thing that I could process over and over was- who does that?

Once I got beyond the shock of it, I asked my wife what could I do? She told me that the young woman needed a bike. Not being able to get to work would compound her already difficult situation.

What I learned early in my career was not just about helping others. I learned about "surprise-and-delight." Surprise-and-delight is about making things memorable. Surprise-and-delight is about the ability to invoke change and get others to change the way they think about their role, their leaders, and even humanity- okay, the last one might be a stretch, but I cannot emphasize how important this is. So, demonstrating compassion for me showed up in the way of surprise-and-delight.

Of course, I believed the right thing to do in this situation was to buy Rose a bicycle. I learned that it is not always about the act of kindness; it is about how to deliver it. In other words, the surprise alone does not do it; it is also the delight.

We bought a bicycle for Rose, put it in the back of the SUV, and off we went to the store. We made sure that Rose was working, and we went in and said hello and asked Rose to come outside. We then presented her with the new bike. Of course, she was shocked and overwhelmed with emotion... and so were we. She was such a beautiful human being who did not deserve to be stepped on by other people. We knew that we could not erase the negative wake left by her ex-boyfriend, but we knew that we could create our own positive wake with her.

It was an awesome day.

What others saw was the gift of the bicycle. What we were giving Rose was the gift of hope. What we were also doing was giving other people hope. We believed that those who worked with her would be inspired and do something special for someone else.

This is why compassion is so relevant. Compassion can create change without even attempting to create change.

Compassion can change the way people think about change and, specifically, change processes.

Take the example of talent planning. Mostly, the talent planning processes in organizations are a very arduous task involving many spreadsheets and boxes to put people in, and oh, a lot of hoops to jump through before people get promoted. That is why I have always believed in the "battlefield promotion."

The battlefield promotion is the anti-succession planning tool. Well, not really, but it is undoubtedly more emotion than process. The battlefield promotion is about taking what we already know about someone, taking a chance on them, and doing it in a meaningful way. Of course, if it is the right person, then the risk is ultimately low. However, the activity of the battlefield promotion is not about following the standard protocol. It is about seizing the opportunity to create a memorable moment in someone's life... while also promoting them.

I have only done this three times in my career. That is because it has to be authentic, and it has to feel right. In my final role at Starbucks, I promoted someone to their first director role.

The battlefield promotion has essential elements: it must be done face-to-face, it must be done in the presence of others-either the person's team or their peers- and, of course, it must take them by total surprise.

At the core of the battlefield promotion is compassion. Most of us have seen examples of how hard people have worked to get promoted, only to see it not happen, not happen soon enough, or they had to sacrifice too much personally to make it happen, like relocating... or worse.

Perhaps the most annoying aspect of talent planning is the TLA (time-limited-assignment). I am strongly against this maneuver and have made my position clear on this in every organization I have worked. My apologies, I must digress and expand on this. This is really important.

Time-limited-assignments have been introduced in many

organizations to address specific situations. Frankly, I believe there are only two situations in which the TLA is viable:

- To cover for an employee that is on a lengthy leave of absence where someone needs to be in charge of the team
- To lead a team when a new leader is hired, but needs time to train and get acclimated to the organization

That is it. Any other reason is a short-cut, a lazy approach to talent planning, an opportunity to pass the ownership of talent planning to the employee instead of senior leadership owning some of it. The TLA became a running joke in one of the organizations that I worked for- everyone had done a TLA. That should not happen.

Okay, here is why I am ranting about TLAs:

Initiating a conversation with a long-term, high rated employee of the company, when there is an open position at the next level, and telling them that you would like for them to take on a TLA is basically saying, "we like the job you have done, we want to test out an opportunity for you in the next role and see what happens. We kind of believe in you, but we want to be sure." That is weak as hell. You cannot get more wishy-washy than that. I mean, show some courage as a leader. Look the person that you already know well in the eyes and say, "We love the work you have done, we are invested in you, we trust you and we are promoting you- congratulations!"

Is that so hard? Just be firm and confident and take a risk. After all, someone took a risk on each of us at some point in our career, unless of course you believe that you did it all on your own.

Do not, I repeat, do not let TLAs dominate your culture. If it is happening, do what you can to stop it now. It is a stupid practice that has gotten out of hand. Thank you for indulging me on that rant.

Now, back to the battlefield promotion topic.

As a leader, you should consider all the aforementioned factors and compassionately promote a deserving employee when the opportunity warrants it. The battlefield promotion is not for every promotional situation, but when you do use it, do not allow this moment to be consumed by process.

Lastly, the battlefield promotion evokes emotion, not only in the person being surprised but even in those who witness it.

At Starbucks, I held a meeting in Miami in late January of 2017. I invited a couple of top talent leaders to join our team meeting. It was my scheming at its best- invite someone that I intended to promote in front of what would be her future peers but invite someone else developing to move up to disguise my intentions.

As part of every meeting, I always ensure that there is a discussion about our future talent. This made for a perfect opportunity to present the conversation and talk about one of the future leaders in the room. Of course, I started the conversation as though it was no one in the room. I shared about our first connection, her passion for her job and the company, and mostly, the heart that she had that in some ways may have held her back from opportunities. I felt like she was confident, but perhaps not confident enough. Overall, I thought she was trapped in the vicious cycle of talent planning that so many other people were experiencing- taking on temporary assignments, completing tasks, shadowing next-level leaders, but no real activity designed to create a quantum leap to get her to the next level. That was about to change.

To this point, we had not discussed any timeline on her moving to the next level, although I had taken an interest in her development and supporting her boss in her development plan.

On this day, though, no development plan was needed. I let a couple of people in on the announcement that I was about to make, the HR leader and her boss... and then I did it.

Of course, she was in the room. I surprised her with a promotion to director. It was the job she wanted, and the place that she wanted, and I can say for sure, she was not expecting it.

I do not often talk about what I have done, because leadership and business success is always about the team. However, this was a day and a moment where I drew on my experience with positional power and thought about how I could make a difference.

After all the tears had stopped flowing, I could see the pride in her face validating all the work that she had done to that point mixed with a sigh of relief and somewhat of a level of disbelief.

There is another part to this. I remember what it felt like to get promoted to director. I remember how the zone vice president came into town, spent time with me, and then ultimately sprang this opportunity on me when I had no expectation of this particular job. He was brilliant in his planning and delivery, and I promised to pay that forward someday.

That is compassion.

Back to a comment earlier in this chapter- compassion is a renewable resource. The more you demonstrate it, the more that it becomes a part of you and, in many cases, the more it becomes a part of the people around you. I have no doubt years from now that this leader will be at a vice president level or higher and will do something special for someone else because of her own experiences.

This is why compassion is directly tied to real, sustainable change. You are investing in future behavior to inspire change and inspire others to do the same.

Think about the times in your life when a story moved you. Not only emotionally, but it compelled you to do something. That is real change, and this also demonstrates why change is not a process, change is an emotion.

Okay, one more story about compassion, surprise-and-delight, and change.

I was promoted to a regional vice president at Starbucks in February of 2008. The person I took over for was being promoted and was asked to immediately relocate to the headquarters. Fortunately, we had already established a personal relationship, but we had a total of three days to spend together before he had to ship off and begin his new role.

And so there I sat, on day four in a vice-president role trying to figure out what I am supposed to be doing. It was the job that I always wanted, and now I did not know what to do with it. Sure, I knew how to go out and visit stores, but I knew there was much more to the job.

No sooner than this thought entered my mind, my administrative assistant came in with a stack of mail. Yes, from the mailroom- we still had that in 2008. It was mostly a stack of junk mail related to the industry, but one of the letters was addressed to me. I wondered how anyone even knew that I was in role after only a few days.

It was a letter from a store manager in Rockwall, Texas, a suburb of Dallas. She wrote to me about an issue that she was having with an espresso machine. However, this was not a problem that I had ever dealt with.

In her letter, she explained her dilemma, and I am paraphrasing: "I am the store manager of a store in your region in Rockwall, Texas. My store is a very low volume store, so I operate with only one Verismo (espresso machine). However, my machine broke a couple of weeks ago, and I had to open up a retail espresso machine and use that to make espresso beverages. Please help."

I could not believe what I was hearing. Let me explain why:

To that point, I had not seen a Starbucks location with less than two Verismo machines, most had two, and some even had three. If you only have one, it needs to be in operation at all times, or it is game over. I mean, the espresso machine is literally the heart of the store, and the most common transaction involves espresso in some way.

Even more shocking is that the Verismo machine is about 3 feet wide and about 1.5 feet deep and weighs a couple of hundred pounds. The "retail" espresso machine that she was describing was the kind that you buy in a department store and put on the counter in your kitchen at home. Consider this visual- the equivalent of replacing a real oven with an easy-bake toy oven. This machine is not meant for commercial use, as her store, even with low volume, could pull a couple of hundred shots a day.

I appreciate her effort to make it work, but it was clear that we had failed her miserably. She was exasperated. I focused less on who had failed her and instead turned my attention to solving the problem... or better said, solving for solutions.

This happened to be the same week that Howard Schultz returned as CEO. We introduced a new espresso machine, the Mastrena, and Howard decided to create an espresso contest to determine who would get them first. Conveniently, I had a store selected as one of the winning locations for the Mastrena machines making their Verismo machines available. This is where surprise-and-delight comes in. Now that I had two Verismo machines that were no longer needed at that location, they could be delivered to the Rockwall store.

I called the regional director and the head of facilities to resolve the matter. However, my direction to them was not to do this in the simple manner that we do everything else.

Instead, my direction was to get the two Verismo machines, put a big red bow on each of them, find out when the store manager would be at the store, and then show up and surprise her. Sneaky, I know.

Well, they did just that, and it worked spectacularly. Not only did this store manager get a replacement machine, she got two... just in case!

A week later, I received another letter in the mail thanking me. Enclosed with the letter was a picture of the store manager and her district manager posing with her new machine. I posted that picture on the corkboard in my office as a reminder of what it means to be a leader, to demonstrate compassion, to change the way people do their work, and feel about their work... to simply make change.

As I pen this chapter and recall this story, the picture sets in my new office- four offices and twelve years later.

Real, sustainable change is bolstered by demonstrating leadership, inspiration, and yes, compassion. Compassion helps others accept change because they see how invested you are in the change.

Compassion is not a given when it comes to change. Frankly, there are some leaders who believe that compassion can be a sign of weakness. All I will say about that is this: I assure you that those you are leading, and who are struggling with change, view compassion as a welcome sight.

No matter where you stand on change and even with these feel-good stories and all the other techniques discussed in this book, change can be challenging and sometimes elusive.

In the end, you will likely still find yourself challenged with one of the most difficult aspects of change- resistance.

CHAPTER 13:

The Resistance

"Change is never painful, only the resistance to change is painful" ~ Gautama Buddha.

This chapter is about taking inventory and taking notes. Everything in this chapter will not apply to someone, but something in this chapter will apply to everyone. Given the change situation you are undertaking, this chapter identifies many reasons people resist change and how you can counteract that resistance.

By the way, this does not only apply to organizational change. Resistance is just as critical to change that you are attempting to implement in your personal life- relationships, parenting, etc.

I covered this earlier in the book. These questions will surface again when resistance appears, especially in a leadership role:

"This is the way it's always been done."

"Things are fine the way that they are."
"If it is not broke, don't fix it."
"We tried that before, and it didn't work."

These eight-word statements often cause less confident and less competent leaders to fold up like a tent under the pressure of implementing change and ultimately overcoming resistance.

After every effort has been made, there will still be those who resist change. No matter how you present the change, it is not for them. Present it nicely, present it harshly- it does not matter, some will still resist.

The reality, though, is that resistance is a part of the change process and resistance to change is one of the biggest stumbling blocks in change management.

It is simply human nature to attempt to counteract any change and maintain the status quo.

Resistance to change may be either overt or implicit. For example, employees may react overtly to a change in policies with outright rejection and protests.

However, they may also refrain from showing disapproval expressly by implicitly not accepting the changes. Managers must understand these problems and help their employees adopt these changes smoothly.

Fortunately, though, dealing with resistance to change is not impossible; however, to properly deal with resistance, we first must understand it. There is a lot to unpack here so, let us explore it.

First, you should anticipate that with any change, there will be some level of resistance. The only question will be how apparent and intense the opposition is.

Second, one of the most significant challenges is that resistance can be contagious. When others see resistance to change, they may believe that it creates an opportunity for them also to resist the change. That said, how you handle resistance as a leader is critically important to the change process because everyone else is watching... always watching.

Resistance can be an individual sport. What I mean by that is there could be as many reasons why change is resisted as there are people on your team or people involved in the change. Solving one root cause of change resistance does not guarantee that you have solved change resistance in total. So, it is impossible to cover all the potential reasons for resistance, but let us talk about some of the reasons why people resist change:

Misunderstanding About The Need For Change

If your team does not clearly understand the need for change, you can expect resistance. If your team feels like the change is being introduced for the sake of change, they will likely not feel compelled to embrace it.

In many instances, this is the main reason for resistance and an obstacle that must be overcome for change to occur. If the very reason for the change is fumbled, you will have little chance of success at implementing the change. It is simply a hurdle that must be cleared.

Misunderstanding is a risk when information is passed on from one leader to another. The translation can change, and, subsequently, people hear a different reason for the change when it finally gets down the line. Even more of a risk is when people hear no reason at all- this may entice them to simply make up their own reason in the absence of hearing one.

Of course, in all things leadership, the reason why should always be known and presented to the team. When it comes to change management, it is even more critical.

Misunderstanding is more than this, though. It is also the factor of what is in it for them. Introducing change that is bottom-line focused and that benefits senior leadership financially may be misunderstood by front-line employees. Those employees may not like the reason for the change because they do not see the same financial benefit for themselves- that is not all that surprising. However, misunderstanding might occur simply because the terminology and the business acumen are so different from top to bottom in an organization that the expectations may create a chasm between front-line employees and senior management.

Close the loop on misunderstanding. If you do not, brace for impact.

Lack Of Trust

When people do not trust that the organization can competently manage the change, there will likely be resistance.

Let me back up. People must first believe in the leader. Only then will they trust the change or vision of change that is being presented.

Introducing the most incredible ideas in the world without leadership trust may be successful, but only to a point. This is an opportunity for you to reflect as a leader about the level of trust you have built ahead of the change process.

Understanding that trust is typically built over time and the more time invested, the more likely is the acceptance of change. Lack of trust must always be considered when you are a new leader leading a team or a leader guiding a newly assembled team.

Lack of trust is not just about people, though. It is also about the change, the ideas themselves. If there is no belief that the change is being done in the best interest of critical stakeholders, skepticism arises, and you can be sure that there will be a lack of trust.

Trust issues are not exclusive to implementing change. As a leader, you should know whether there are trust gaps and address those even when change is not being implemented.

Lack Of Competence

Fear of whether a person can execute the change is something that many people experience but will not often admit during the change process. In general, no one wants to admit that they cannot get the job done. Not knowing if you can make the transition very well will turn some away from attempting to make the change.

Sweeping changes on the job can cause your team members to doubt their capabilities to perform their duties. Your team members may be resisting these changes because they are worried that they cannot adapt to new work requirements.

Testing for understanding is an integral part of leadership. This is critically important in organizations where there are long-tenured employees. One of the risks of tenure is that people are assumed to know what they are doing after being around for an extended period. It becomes an assumptive process on both ends- the leader assumes knowledge, and the employee assumes they cannot ask for help out of fear of being viewed as incompetent. It is a potentially vicious cycle.

It may make people uncomfortable in the short term to ask them to demonstrate competency. Still, over time it will make them more confident, likely feel more valued because you showed care, and you may get the change implemented even more effectively.

It helps to not single people out when attempting to test for competency. Some people you assume to be competent might be the ones that you should be testing for understanding, so it makes sense to include everyone.

By the way, lack of competency cuts both ways. If employees view the leader as incompetent, do not bother with the change-it will not be accepted. I am just being real.

One more thing, if you doubt your competency as the leader, there is a good chance that your team does too.

Not Being Involved In The Process

Whether it is prudent or appropriate, if people are not part of the change, change can come as a surprise, and resistance can appear. People like to know what is going on- it helps break down the hierarchical nature of an organization.

One other benefit- bringing people along on the process may help you identify blind spots- those areas where you are at risk because the change leaders have not done the job below them, have not done the job below them in a long time, or the role has changed over time.

Informed employees tend to have higher engagement scores than uninformed employees, so the benefit is more far-reaching than just the change you are looking to implement.

Fear Of The Unknown

Routine is a comforting word for many people. When patterns are broken, fear can enter the equation. Fear then creates resistance. Fear assumes the change is going to be bad for them.

Organizational change, in many cases, leads to uncertainty and some dose of fear. It is normal for people to feel the fear of uncertainty. When employees feel uncertainty in the process of transformation, they think of change as a threat.

As a leader, addressing fears is essential in the change process. You may be thinking, how will I know what they fear? You have to ask. Even if you ultimately cannot get employees to disclose those fears, it does not preclude you from having the responsibility to ask. The good news is that they may enlighten you with something that you would have never suspected was a fear risk. Again, more blind spots being exposed.

Fear is an immensely powerful emotion. I would be sure not to ignore it in the change process.

Change Means More Work

New things usually mean more work. Even if it is the same amount of work, it will likely take more time and feel like more time while working through the change process.

Do not underestimate the amount of frustration that can come from people slowing down in accomplishing their work. You may experience this more from your long-tenured or most competent employees. This frustration can lead to job dissatisfaction and if there is one group that you do not want to lose are your high performers. If there is another group that you do not want to lose are those who have institutional knowledge.

I do not recommend that you ever take on the role of salesperson during the change process. Still, it may be worth some investment of time driving home the finer points when people feel like they are doing unnecessary work to get the same result they were getting before. The good news is that this stage may not last long, and they will soon see the benefit of what you are introducing.

Obtain Buy-In At All Levels

Buy-in is critical to obtaining support. And the more support you have, the less resistance there is. Not only do you need to find ways to get buy-in from your team, but you must also get it from executives. Change programs strategically crucial for business have a higher probability of success when you obtain support from the top. Executives think from a top-down perspective. They look at the organization, its bottom line, and its strategic direction. Put that mindset first, and you will stand a greater chance of overcoming executive resistance.

Buy-in at the executive level is essential because mid-level managers looking to implement change without an executive sponsor are at risk of faulty execution. When executive sponsors do not buy-in, it becomes apparent to others that this change is not that important and responsibility to implement it wanes. Also, to go 180 degrees to the other side of this, you need executives to be educated and demonstrate buy-in to articulate the change.

Organizational Politics

Some resist change as a political strategy to demonstrate that the decision is wrong. It is a fundamental belief or principle on which the resistor is standing. At times, you look for more reason behind their stance, and there is not one- they are simply an I-am-right-and-you-are-wrong person.

They may also resist showing that the person leading the change is not up to the task. Perhaps, it is someone that believes that they should have been promoted into that position. They may be just armchair quarterbacks that second-guess every decision that every leader makes.

Others may resist because they believe that they will lose some power in the organization. Giving up something or losing something can power their disdain for the change resulting in the person taking organizational, political action.

In all these instances, these individuals are committed to seeing the change effort fail.

Political obstacles are frustrating when you are trying to

implement needed change. I would recommend taking this issue on directly as an act of treason. Yes, I know it is too strong of a word choice... but it needs to be addressed. Remember that this is a person who is spending more time thinking about how to sabotage the change than you are spending time trying to prevent them from stopping the change.

Faulty Implementation Approach

Sometimes it is not what a leader does, but it is how he or she does it that creates resistance to change. Undue resistance can occur because changes are introduced in an insensitive manner or entirely at the wrong time.

In other words, people may agree with the change that you want to implement, but they may not agree with how you are going about making the change.

Timing can be everything when it comes to change, but it is somewhat of a guess when you are crafting a timeline that is months out. Change implementation is optimized when you find that window of time to grab the most attention, or in corporate terms, the most mindshare.

Poor Previous Experience With Change

Most employees already have some experience with a previous organizational change process. If those experiences were negative, they may believe that this change will not be easy either. So, these experiences can cause resistance to change.

Even individuals who claim to enjoy change may find it challenging in the workplace. After all, choosing to change one's personal life is different from accepting top-down organizational change. Resistance to change in the workplace occurs because employees often do not have a choice, which can trigger a sense of lost control and uncertainty.

Too often, employees focus on what may be lost, rather than what can be gained. In this situation, there may be a benefit to asking direct questions when the rollout is occurring. You may be able to break through those barriers related to this before it is too late.

I have only identified ten reasons of many reasons why people resist change. Now, let us discuss how you overcome them. Again, overcoming resistance to change is not easy, but it is possible.

It will take leadership diligence and awareness. It will also require you to deploy some strategies that help you keep the change process on course. Below are a few to consider:

Communication

The first strategy to overcome resistance to change is to communicate. Communication is vital, but you already knew that. However, part of the key to success is two-way communication.

You, as a leader preaching change to your team, will only get you so far. While there are messages that you must communicate as part of the change process, try letting your employees initiate the conversation. People want to be heard and giving them a chance to voice their opinions will help alleviate their frustration over the impending change.

You may also find that your people will share concerns, suggestions, and information that reveals clues that may help you adjust how you will lead through the change. At the very least, understanding them will help you pinpoint the root cause of employee resistance to change.

I know this sounds basic, but most leaders like to talk more than they listen or, at the very least, talk before they listen.

Think about communication from this perspective: When organizations conduct roundtable meetings or even engagement surveys, you never really hear employees tell you that you are communicating too much- it is usually just the opposite.

Most studies show that it takes multiple attempts at communication before your message even gets through. Think about it the other way around- if you rarely hear from your employees, even when you do, the message may not resonate with you. You need to hear it more often so that it will stick.

I also believe that you can garner a higher level of respect by clarifying that your objective in the communication process is to seek understanding, not agreement. This distinction is essential as you do not want to send false hope by asking for feedback and others believing their feedback will be heard and acted upon. The emphasis is on ensuring that they are listened to.

At the same time, it is asserting your role as a leader and the need to make tough decisions that may not always be popular and agreeable while ensuring that people are still being heard.

Share The Reasons For Change

The next strategy to overcome resistance to change is to communicate the Why, What, and How. The communication plan you develop must be more than just telling your employees what you want them to do. Effective communication makes the information relevant for each segment of your workforce, focusing on what they care about and need to know— telling your team about the What and How is important, telling them the Why is critical.

Why breaks through and answers many of the questions that your employees have, questions that are almost always tied to resistance. Sharing the Why also helps those leaders on your team, when you have layers of leadership, to effectively communicate further down, increasing the chances of change adoption.

What ensures clarity of what you are going after, your intent, and the intended outcome. What is particularly important as you want to ensure that you solve the right problem and that everyone knows what problem you want to solve. I know, seems basic- you may be surprised what people miss.

How ensures that you have given the team the tools to be successful with the change. The only thing more challenging than dealing with the resistance to change is failing because you simply left it to chance that everyone knew how you wanted it done... and they did not know.

Get Excited

Your energy level will affect the energy level of the team- do not underestimate this. Even if the team is already energized, you can still raise their energy level. If the team is not energized, you play a critical role in bringing their energy level up.

This should be authentic- if you genuinely believe in the change, and authentically communicate the energy behind the change, your conviction will be evident amongst the group, and they will follow your lead. Any hesitancy will be detected and ultimately increase the likelihood of change resistance.

This is not to be confused with cheerleading- which can sometimes be nomenclature for style over substance or artificial excitement.

Honestly, if you are not excited about the change, then do not lead the change. However, if you are genuinely enthusiastic about the change, do not hold back.

Do Your Homework

Finally, understand the change inside and out. Investing time to talk to subject matter experts, testing out the change personally, understanding the risk, and understanding the available solutions is critical. And of course, be confident when it comes time to deliver the change.

In a well-executed change process, the leader needs to show up, in some respects, like a referee in sports. Everyone knows that you are there, you are in charge of the action, but you never want to become the topic of conversation.

Doing your homework puts you in a position of being the subject matter expert, which will exude confidence from your team.

From there, you are on your way to real, sustainable change.

CHAPTER 14:

Putting It All Together

With everything that you have read in this book, like most things in life, implementation comes down to execution; such is true with real, sustainable change. However, the information I have shared in this book will be difficult to execute unless you break through all the deep-seated barriers that people hold onto when change is introduced.

By the way, that means starting with yourself. So, I took my own advice.

I have been on a personal journey of change for as long as I can remember. I do not mean taking life as it comes and reacting to it: I mean taking steps to change the trajectory of my life. And yet, I have made as many poor personal decisions related to health, family, friendships, work, etc. as the next person. You name it, I have been challenged with it.

I also discovered that I was not the change-agent that I thought I was. In fact, I was relatively conservative and could not plant a flag on any real significant risk that I had taken. I must admit, that stung a bit, but as it has been said, you can lie to others, but you cannot lie to yourself.

Nonetheless, I forged on every day to be better and change for the better. This revelation did cause me to take some risks, to plant some flags. Writing a book was one of them. Changing careers was another one.

As there was a personal motivation for writing my previous book, 'The Power Of Or: Choosing And Doing What Matters Most,' there is a personal story about why I decided to write this book too.

At the beginning of the book, I mentioned: "The moment that a moment is gone, change has occurred."

This is as simple as looking out the window at a building while driving along the highway. You glance back at it three seconds later, and it is gone- that is how fast change occurs.

Why this point strikes me so poignantly is that we can never get that moment back. Fortunately, we can reflect on it through video and pictures, but you cannot re-create it or change it once it has happened.

I know that I am not telling you anything new here, but I am sharing it because we spend so much time focused on the significant changes in our lives, yet the millions of constant, small changes tend to shape our lives just as much, sometimes even more. So, what to do with this?

I will share what I did with this.

In 2019, as I was writing my first book, I arrived at a place where the framework of the book was complete, but I could not put the pieces together.

I knew that I needed something else, some new form of inspiration to move from the place where I was to the next place to finish the writing journey.

Enter Mitch Telson.

I asked Mitch to write the preface to this book because of the mentorship he provided to me over the last eighteen years. However, I also asked Mitch to introduce this book because of the impact that he has had on my life personally.

Let me tell you about Mitch, share a bit about how we met, and then share the relevance about his impact on my leadership journey and the journey to change.

In early 2019, after my mother died, I experienced my first bout with writer's block. Understandably so, it was a bit difficult to focus.

It was time to take a break from it all. About that time, I received a call from Mitch Telson. He always had the uncanny timing to reach out just when I needed it. We had been talking about getting together for years, and now was the time. Mitch said to visit him in Santa Barbara, and so I did. My wife and I made a trip to California to spend time with Mitch and his wife. The entire trip was memorable and relaxing, unlike any vacation we had in years. The most memorable thing about our trip was being at the house with Mitch and his wife Jeffyne... with their fifteen giant tortoises, nine collies, and at least thirty cats- I might be off on the cat count, and I may have missed an extra critter or two.

What Mitch and his wife Jeffyne have done to rescue dogs, collies in particular for Mitch and many, many cats with Jeffyne's rescue organization is extraordinary. Explaining it in a book will not do it justice, but that is all I can do for this narrow print communication vehicle. Whatever your imagination can create in your mind about the sanctuary that Mitch and his wife have made, I promise you that it is even better than that in person, and I promise to do this story justice in a future writing.

From this trip to Santa Barbara, I learned nothing and everything. This is true of all my connections with Mitch. There was no specific conversation about any particular topic, yet I walked away with what I needed to focus on finishing the book. I only had two readers for the first book, and Mitch was one of them. The other reader was Cos LaPorta, who is an equally remarkable human being that I will be calling on in the future to help tell my story. I credit Cos for the last chapter of my first book. He had great insight into what was needed to round out the story.

Back to Mitch. One piece of advice he gave me stuck with me and really helped me on my literary journey. Mitch said that writing a book must be treated as a job- literally, clock in and out. Now, he was referencing the journey of his wife writing a book, but it played directly into my situation. That struck a nerve with me because I was treating writing a book like writing a book- it just was not the same energy that I would exact if I were in a job. Being off from work for a year, I had conditioned myself to be leisurely about writing the book. So, that was a significant takeaway. From there, I returned home, I "clocked in," and my writing began to flow.

Also, I recall getting back home from my trip to Santa Barbara and sending Mitch the manuscript of the book on a Sunday evening. By Monday evening, he had already read 59 pages giving me feedback. Classic Mitch.

I have one more story to share about the character of Mitch Telson.

I was working for Starbucks in Dallas, Texas, somewhere around 2010. At that time, Mitch was doing some consulting work for a company in Dallas and was just passing through. He called me to get together, but our schedules did not work out on that trip. However, on the last day that Mitch was in town, he called me back and let me know that he was leaving. Instead of jumping on a plane and taking a direct flight back to Santa Barbara, Mitch had been notified of a collie that needed to be rescued. Mitch abandoned his flight plan, rented a car, drove to Houston, Texas to pick up the collie, and then went all the way back to Santa Barbara, California, with the pooch in tow. Who does that?

It made me reflect on the person I am and the person I want to be.

That is Mitch Telson. So, on to how we met.

When I first met Mitch Telson, I had just arrived at my first corporate office job.

This was my first senior director role, so I had a corner window office. That sounds great, but I did not get to enjoy it for the first six months. It was early 2002, and we were still on extremely high alert as a country after 9/11. None of us could get the image of the planes hitting the Twin Towers out of our heads... and... I could not get the image out of my head of the planes coming into Love Field airport in Dallas that had a flight plan that took them around our building, Renaissance Tower. That is correct; about every eight minutes, another plane would come around the corner and appear to be headed straight for our building and really, straight for my office.

I could not do it. I had to go work at an interior cubicle. The irony of it- you work all those years to get a corner office and cannot work in it.

My life had changed in every possible way. I did not feel comfortable knowing where to park in the parking garage, where to eat during lunchtime, or even what floor to go to for the next meeting on my calendar. I was lost in my new role.

I share all of that to say that I was in the most awkward stage of my professional career to that point. I was in change overload. It was during this time that I was introduced to Paxil and Wellbutrin. For those that are not familiar, that is not the name of a corporate law firm- these are anxiety medications. I did not expect that I would have hand tremors at the age of 34. Stress can kill- not just a slogan.

My first role in the office was to take on a full scale, national project called Project Store. I had been notified that I would be working with external business consultants from McKinsey- that was new for me.

McKinsey was one of the big three consulting companies in the country. It would be unfair to characterize how McKinsey works in 2020, but I can tell you in 2002, McKinsey very much resembled the movie called "The Firm" starring Tom Cruise... and that is not a compliment.

Eight McKinsey associates were working on this engagement, including two engagement managers. The six that were directly involved with the Project Store work all fit the profile. They graduated from the best business schools all over the country, places like Wharton. The youngest one was probably 24 years old, and the oldest one was 28 years old. Only one of them was married, and he appeared to continually receive "The Firm"-type pressure when he did not want to work 18 hours a day as what appeared to be required, I mean recommended by McKinsey.

Then, there was a plot twist.

As we gathered for the first project engagement meeting, in walked the McKinsey consultants. The image of "The Right Stuff," the stroll of the astronauts, was the only way to describe it. A confident group walking in to take over the company. Not really, but yes.

Through the other meeting room door walked a gentleman, mid-50's, long ponytail, and an earring. I was not sure who he was and why he was crashing our meeting. Then I learned that he was the "other" consultant... Mitch Telson.

When people say do not underestimate leadership, I had a real-life experience that proves that. McKinsey may have come with an army of people and resources, but throughout the year engagement on Project Store, I learned far more from Mitch- about business for sure, but also about life. As it turns out, they do not, cannot teach that at Wharton.

Mitch and I made a trip to Chicago together, and it was one of my most valuable leadership learning experiences. Most interesting is that if you ask me what I learned from Mitch my answer may not be what you would expect. My response to that question would be the same as when I flew to Santa Barbara last year- I learned nothing and everything simultaneously.

The time together also taught me a lot about mentoring. Mentoring does not need to be this overengineered process to be successful and help others on their journey. Storytelling helps, and Mitch had stories to tell.

So, that is a bit about Mitch and about how we met. I will come back to his impact on my leadership journey.

Now, back to my personal journey of change.

For me, part of understanding change was accepting that it was always going to happen. It felt like the minute that I got used to something in life; it changed. The older that I got, I began to realize that more change was occurring.

There was a crucial pivot in my life- when I stopped resisting change and began accepting it, my life turned around. When I stopped just accepting change and decided to make change work for me, my life was transformed. When I decided to transform my life, I began to see the world in a much clearer way, and that allowed me to go to the next level, which was that I began to help others transform their life. This progression did not happen all in one day or from one event, but hundreds of small revelations over weeks, months, and years.

My personal journey of change really began at age four. I know that sounds silly, but there were very profound things that happened during that time that are etched in my memory forever. Things that I began to witness and understand shaped my view of the world- spending almost the entire time of age four alone at home, followed by my parent's divorce the next year, and my mother shooting my father in the stomach the year after that. Oh, and then the following year, age seven, breaking my right arm.

Unfortunately, I was right-handed in everything that I did. The break was so severe that I was in traction with my arm over my head for more than a month! I must admit, I had impeccable timing. As the thirty-day hospital stay lined up, it meant that I spent both Thanksgiving and Christmas in the hospital.

Honestly, that did break my spirit a bit- okay, it broke my spirit a lot. The limitations of lying in traction for that long meant that my equilibrium was totally gone, and, standing up for the first time, I realized that I had to learn to walk again, Seriously? I am seven years old with a broken arm that had just healed, and now I have to learn how to walk again? It seemed cruel.

However, I still found a way to change it into something positive. I learned to write with my left hand, and I also learned how to play basketball with my left hand. As a result, I remained ambidextrous in a number of activities.

This experience was about taking change and using it to take me somewhere else better. No, I will not tell you that I understood that level of insight at age seven because I did not. Like every other seven-year-old boy, I wondered what was for lunch and who I would beat playing marbles after school.

What I did understand was that life goes on, and, other than a few close family members and some incredible nurses, no one knew or cared that I thought I might never ride a bike or play basketball again. Life is not always kind or balanced. I had to gather myself and find the fortitude to move forward.

At the age of nine, I learned about being an entrepreneur. I had my first newspaper route. I then sold newspaper subscriptions door-to-door at age eleven and mowed lawns starting at age thirteen.

We lived in ten homes in ten years from third grade until I graduated high school.

Those are some of the changes from my younger years, but I do not want to focus there.

The real transformation began when I started formally working. I went to work at Wendy's shortly after I turned 16. I worked there for a couple of years.

While everyone else complained about it, I thrived. Work is work, and I am getting paid. I get free food too. I mean, what could be better than this?

As I progressed through my career, I worked for a clothing store company through high school and college. A critical moment came when I left there and went to work for a large mass merchant, who I would learn later was on their way out of business. I absolutely hated that job! They paid me a lot of money to go to work there... and that would be the only time in my career that I would chase money.

Working for the mass merchant, I learned about change in that role because most leaders there did not know how to lead change.

Many of them were grizzled and frustrated older men who should have been doing something else, anything else but that job. At 23, I found myself wanting to change the world, and these leaders were not having it. I learned valuable lessons in a short time. I knew that I would not work there for long, but I did not expect it to be less than three months. So, off I went.

If you wanted to find change in the 1990s, Blockbuster Video was the spot! Think about it; they were changing their new release wall every single week with new movies- every week for fourteen years for me.

I found my happy place working in a video store. I only spent two years of my career working in a store, but even working in higher-level roles, I went back to spend as much time as I could where it all started, where movies always remained sacred.

I missed working in the stores. I enjoyed my other broad roles, but I rejected the politics of them. For my achievements, I was given the corner office job in the headquarters.

I took my office badge from Blockbuster and framed it and placed it directly in front of my desk on the wall of my home office so that I could always see it and always be reminded of the experience.

Whether it was the volume of change, the frequency of change, or the intensity of change, I vowed to learn from that experience.

I realized that I could no longer allow change to happen to me- I had to be more aggressive than the change. I had to outthink it. Mostly though, full mastery for me would be the ability to lead change.

The last few years at Blockbuster were difficult for obvious financial and competitive reasons, but the teams that I led found ways to deliver best-in-class results, and we learned to harness change. There were never discussions about what we could not do; only energy focused on how we could do it.

I then had a spectacular 11-year career working for Starbucks. Whatever I could have dreamed would happen during that time happened. So many great memories and relationships were built.

I do recall needing Mitch's counsel when I was presented with an opportunity that would mean leaving Starbucks. This serves as an example of how Mitch has positively impacted my life. His wisdom has guided me through many difficult decisions.

It was early 2017, and Jamba Juice had come calling. I had received many calls from many recruiters in the two years prior but had balked at all of them. I mean, leaving Starbucks? I can talk about change all day long, but that was change that was beyond my comprehension. I did change companies eleven years prior when I left Blockbuster to join Starbucks, but hell, who would not have given the trajectory of each company at the time. This was not that- Starbucks was still doing remarkably well at the time.

Mitch had done a better job of staying connected to me than I had done staying connected to him. Over the years, he had called me about potential leadership roles and board roles and had been available to talk whenever I needed him. That is a real mentor.

So, we discussed the opportunity. The question that resonated the most from our conversation was a relatively simple one: Mitch asked, "if the next Starbucks role could be in Texas instead of Seattle, would I still consider this role at Jamba Juice?" That question awakened my senses. It made me think about why I was considering the decision to leave. It also made me think about change and how much risk I was willing to take. I am not going to say that I took the COO role at Jamba Juice just to challenge myself at taking a chance, but it definitely played into it.

Again, I could talk about change all day long, but if I was not willing to make change in my personal life, I am not sure how far I would go to make change happen as a leader— reality check.

As with much of life's journey, if I had not taken that chance, I would likely not be sitting here writing this book about change. Everything is connected.

I have learned to appreciate 'those days' when I wake up, and I can say that my health is good, my family is good, my personal relationships are good, my work is good, my financial situation is good, my sports teams are winning and I am doing something that I choose to do- that is a really, really good day.

As it turns out, life is very unpredictable, and it becomes difficult at times to find one of 'those days.' I don't gamble, but I suppose that it is like pulling the lever on a slot machine with seven slot options (I am not sure that there are machines with that many symbols that come up at once- hence, I know nothing about gambling) and getting all seven to come up with the same symbols. The odds are low, but the important part is that it is possible. Our level of success with processing change and leading change may be increasing our odds of having one of 'those days' more than we know.

Leading through change or working through personal change is not easy. There are many deep-seated barriers to breakthrough. That said, accepting change, inspiring others to accept change, and understanding how to spot and respond to resistance to change can unlock incredible possibilities for you as a leader and even on your personal journey.

Just remember: "Change is not a process- change is an emotion."

Approaching change in this manner will liberate you from process and get you closer to the human aspect of change. Other humans will appreciate that. Now, go make that change.

CPSIA information can be obtained
at www.ICGtesting.com
Printed in the USA
BVHW091043080921
615287BV00014B/92/J

9 780578 241944